How To Analyze People

Improve Your Influencing and Persuasion Skills by Reading the Body Language and Mind-Control Techniques

Dale McLeo

Table of Contents

Introduction

As humans, we communicate our feelings and intentions in more ways than we are even aware of. Whether it's through speech, writing, body language, or even a sudden change in our usual choices, being able to interpret such information correctly is an advantage that should not be ignored. It, in fact, makes us powerful when we can decipher the mood, intent, and desires of those we communicate with.

It is to this end that this book, ***How To Analyze People***, was written. Whether you are on stage, casually conversing with a friend or interviewing someone for a job, the methods in this book will be of immense benefit to you.

In addition to being able to analyze people, this book also reveals proven methods to influence and control the thoughts and actions of anyone. And by proven, that means there is nothing fictional about the mind-control methods shared in this book. Who wouldn't want to learn such a skill?

Chapter 1: What is Verbal Communication?

There are no fixed rules on how people transmit knowledge and information. In some places and to some people, the use of signs and symbols is the only means known for transferring ideas, information or knowledge. Verbal communication is the most known means of conveying our thoughts. It is the easiest and the fastest. Verbal communication is an oral or written communication wherein an individual or group of people communicates with another individual or group of persons with the use of words. It is a means of communication wherein the person who wishes to transmit information or knowledge does so by clothing their feelings, thoughts, and observations with words. This communication could be in the form of arguments, discussions, presentations, meetings, and so on. The crux of this is that whatever the communicator feels or thinks is let out through words.

The effectiveness of verbal communication is mainly dependent on the communicator. In verbal communication, the speaker is expected to be mindful of their expressions, volume of voice, tone, speed, and so on. A speaker communicating verbally is expected to speak with a high tone and with clarity. It is important that the audience not only hear the speaker but also they should be able to perfectly understand what ideas the speaker is trying to convey. A speaker, speaking verbally, is also expected to bear in mind the nature of his audience while communicating. Connecting with the audience is key, and it helps to ensure that what was intended to be passed down has been passed down. The exact intentions of the speaker must be understood by the audience, vividly. This is particularly possible by ensuring that as a speaker you get feedback from your audience.

The feedback from the audience need not be oral. The feedback could exist in the form of nods by the audience, or their rapt attention to what is being said or the manner of questions asked after or during the communication. Either way, this feedback helps the speaker to know how well they are communicating with their audience. The tone and speed used in a presentation, meeting or speech are not the same as that used in an argument or debate. The response of the recipient is usually instant in verbal communication, this owing to the fact that the sending and receiving of information between the communicator and listener is simultaneous. The effectiveness of verbal communication is also dependent on the listening ability of the speaker to the listener and their attentiveness to details.

Many are quick to assume that verbal communication deals only with spoken words, but this is not so. Verbal communication is the use of language to communicate, and this communication could be both by writing and speaking. What you are now reading is a piece of written, verbal information. Through the pages of this book, we have verbal communication. Oral is not only associated with the words of mouth but also with written words. Verbal communication is any form of communication with words, while nonverbal communication does not involve the use of words. This could be the use of gestures, silence, or other movements. Some people clap, snap their fingers, or tap a part of their body to communicate. Usually, this is coded between the communicator and recipient, who both might not want people around them to figure out what is being conveyed. If you cried, laughed or screamed, you will be sending a message to people around you, but this does not qualify as verbal communication. Both nonverbal communication and verbal communication can be used for exactly the same purpose—sending messages to people around us as to what we think or feel, or our ideas and knowledge—however, both do not communicate using the same means.

Types of Verbal Communication

1. **Intrapersonal verbal communication**: This is a form of verbal communication that is extremely private and restricted. It involves just one person in which both the sender and the receiver of the message joggle roles. These are silent communications we have with ourselves. It could be through soliloquizing or just our thoughts in our heads, or words said out loud to ourselves to

encourage oneself. Either way, the communicator is the recipient of the information, and it is usually private.

2. **Interpersonal verbal communication**: This form of communication involves just two individuals. Here, the role of communicator–the recipient is constantly swapped between the two persons. An interpersonal relationship is also restricted and private because whatever is being discussed is restricted to just the two participants in the discussion even though another can join in subsequently or intermittently.

3. **Small-Group verbal communication**: This involves communication between more than two persons. We find this form of communication in team meetings, group or board meetings, press conferences, and other meetings with a quantifiable number of persons. The requirement here is that the number of persons should not be too large to enable each participant to communicate with the other. Usually, small group communication should be orderly since the persons involved are negligible; however, the communication can become chaotic if the participants do not table out their agenda. Even where an agenda is drawn, it could still become chaotic if not properly organized.

4. **Public verbal communication**: This is the broadest of the four types of communication. It involves a speaker

addressing a large group of people. Election campaigns, manifesto, and so on are all examples of this type of discussion. A lot is required in public communication than in any of the other three types of communication. Some of the skills later discussed might not come in as important in any of the other three, but all the skills should be put to use here. Nonverbal communication is also crucial here too.

Differences Between Verbal and Nonverbal Communication

1. While it would seem that in all we have said verbal communication is more accessible, this will not be the same after we have fully discussed and understood the differences between verbal and nonverbal communication. In the first sense, verbal communication uses a single channel of communication (words). You are either saying a word at a time or saying nothing. You cannot say multiple words at the same time. Also, in communicating verbally, you can only use words and nothing more. This is the basic and only definition of verbal communication–communication with the use of words, whether written or oral. You will learn that while reading this book, you can also be chewing gum with your hand on your head and rolling your eyes at the same time.

This implies that nonverbal communication uses multiple channels of communication. It is communicating at the same time using diverse means. Also, nonverbal communication does not use just one form of communication. It includes eye contact, clapping, shouting, tapping your feet and so on. Unlike verbal communication, which uses just one means to communicate (words), nonverbal communication uses multiple means of communication.

2. Secondly, verbal communication is distinct and linear, whereas nonverbal communication is not. The latter is continuous and relative to context. Usually, words have a defined meaning and a prescribed manner in which they are used. In making a sentence, there are parts of the sentence that must come before the other before it can be deemed grammatically correct. Also, the words proceed in a linear manner. We know that to spell the word "back," you must begin with the letter 'b' and end with the letter 'k.' Not only this, you must proceed in a defined manner so that it can be correct. You cannot spell 'back' as 'back.' For verbal communication, everything is defined and there are rules regulating how words are to be arranged and used in some instances. However, nonverbal communication works according to context. If someone approaches you, laughing and waving, it does not necessarily mean that they have any goodwill toward you,

but this would most likely be interpreted to mean goodwill. There are no definite rules as to communicating under nonverbal communication. Actions and means of communication move according to context, continuously.

3. Verbal communication involves conscious communication, while nonverbal communication is at most times unconscious. It is a given that people think of what to say or write before they do so. Sometimes, we even have to revise over and over again what we want to say beforehand to be sure that we are on track. Particularly, when you have to engage in an organized debate or give a speech, you have to think through what you want to say, when to say it and how to say it. All these are not given in nonverbal communication. When people around you say funny things, you do not have to think about laughing; it comes to you naturally. Sometimes you do not think before engaging in most of your nonverbal communication and, oftentimes, the meaning intended in nonverbal communication is usually misplaced. A look at a person might be misinterpreted from what is intended. It is important to understand that it is not all the time that nonverbal communication is unconscious. If you were going for an interview, you might be conscious about how you choose to stand and stare and even your gesture. The same goes for if you are in a gathering and something funny is said, you might choose not to laugh. The primary

thing to understand is that nonverbal communication can be unconsciously or consciously done, but verbal communication is usually conscious.

4. Another significant difference is that nonverbal communication is mostly universal, while verbal communication is not. It is generally believed that smiling has goodwill and feeling attached to it and that a swearing person should be avoided. However, this is not a general rule because contexts differ, and what a particular nonverbal communication means in one context might in another not be the same. It is a cultural belief that in South Korea, you do not give a person money with just one hand. When we talk of verbal communication, on the other hand, it connotes something that is not general. This is because people differ according to their various cultures, dialects, and way of life so a distinct word could have one meaning in one place and another meaning elsewhere. The major difference is that nonverbal communication is more universally accepted in its usage than verbal communication.

The differences explained above have helped us to better appreciate the need for the skills to effectively communicate verbally, as the features of verbal and nonverbal communication are majorly interwoven and that in most cases one cannot be without the other. As will be gleaned from our next discussion, even though this section is about educating us on what verbal communication is about and the skills needed to better communicate verbally, one cannot have one without the other. It is, therefore, important that we learn how to better communicate nonverbally while also communicating verbally.

Chapter 2: Verbal Communication Skills

It is often said that where hundreds of persons with the same talent are competing for a particular position, then what stands one out from the rest is our interpersonal skills. How do you approach situations? How do you speak? How do you convey your idea to another? All these things matter, especially in a competitive world like ours. We are quickly coming to the realization that it is one thing to know something, and it is an entirely different thing to communicate to the world what we know in a manner that would sell what you know to the public. With time, we begin to realize that as insignificant as we make the little things seem, they all matter. Small things matter, too. This would bring to the reasonable question of what could be done to increase one's verbal communication skills. With just a smile, a free disposition to the manner we pass our messages, a lighter tone, and a stellar method of expression when writing, there is no limit to how excellent our communication could be and how well we would be better at doing what we know how to do best. It is important to note that nothing written under this subhead is intended to give the impression that verbal communication deals only with spoken dialogue. Every skill discussed here covers the full definition already attached to verbal communication above, which is that verbal communication is the transmission of ideas, thoughts, feelings, knowledge, and information with the use of words. Below are some verbal communication skills:

1. **Be friendly in your manner of approach**: As said above, the little things matter. A smile should accompany your manner of communicating. These, of course, should entirely be based on the subject matter of discussion. The primary ingredient required in your communication is for you to be real in the way you communicate with your audience. People are more disposed to listen and accept people who are friendly in the way they interact with people, and are true to such friendliness. It means that being pretentious won't work. Verbal communication can be used in both a formal and informal setting. When you communicate verbally in a formal setting, you might pick on the mood of the environment.

2. **Before you speak, think**: There is a popular saying about keeping quiet when you have nothing to say and leaving everyone to believe that you are a fool than to open your mouth and remove all doubt. This skill is to draw respect with your communication because people will be accustomed to the fact that you do not just speak unreasonably and that you think of what you want to say before you speak. People are more prone to listen to you whenever you eventually speak if you imbibe this skill. This skill does not, however, imply that you should have no opinion of controversial issues. It does not mean that because you feel what you are about to say or write will be dismissed, you should not take a leap. It only means that

before you voice your opinions, they should be worth the ink of your pen or the silver of your mouth.

3. **Be clear when communicating**: Not everyone today has the time or the emotional energy to listen to people speak. If you are one of such people who do not know how to speak without beating around the bush, then you might have to do a lot of thinking before you pen your thoughts, and also before you speak. A person who communicates indirectly never attracts any form of respect, and even if they do, it won't be how they interact. Sometimes, your inability to communicate might stem from the faulted ideology that to be listened to and respected, you must use ambiguous words. We have truly communicated if the recipient understands and appreciates the wealth of our knowledge. No communication has been made by showing off the number of synonyms or antonyms one knows with respect to a particular word. You should aim to leave your audience less confused than when you met them.

4. **Talk less**: There is beauty in brevity. No one likes people who love to dominate others with their words. No one likes people who rattle on and on without giving any space for others to express their views. Learn to be concise and hit the nail on the head when you communicate. Your ability to say a lot in just a few words will be listened to and respected more. The trick here is to understand when

to say less. If what you intend to say can be said with fewer words than you expected, you definitely should take that route.

5. **Be authentic**: Many times, we see people displaying "drama" all in the name of communication. People who believe they cannot effectively communicate without first displaying drama end up merely entertaining their audience without having made a point. Today, more than ever, people are to those who tend to portray to others what they are not. To fully communicate and pass down your information, you should be free, genuine, and transparent. The world you speak to will appreciate you more if you spoke to them from your heart.

6. **Practice respect and humility**: People hold in high esteem those who accord them the same respect or an even higher form of respect. Humility is a modest view of how important you are in a certain place, situation, or within the midst of persons. Speaking to people with a sense of humility and respect spurs them to treat you the same way when they speak to you. Humble people attract people to them. Learning to speak to people respectfully is key in your communication.

7. **Be confident**: When we talk about exuding humility in your communication and then also talk about self-confidence, it doesn't mean that you sacrifice your self-

confidence on the altar of humility. When we talk of confidence, it is the appreciation of one's abilities and talents. Humility, on the other hand, deals with a modest view of those abilities and how they make us different from others. You should be able to appreciate what you have while being modest in your appreciation. This is the perfect way of being self-confident yet humble. It is not enough that you do this; you should exude your humility and let it live through the way you communicate. This can be gleaned from your choice of words, the pitch and tone of your voice, your aptitude in the description, the way you look at your audience and, of course, your body language. There are other determining factors. There's no limit to what you can do to communicate with confidence and humility at the same time.

8. **Mind your body language**: Let's say that your words are the vehicle and your body language is the fuel you need to move the vehicle. Without your body language, your words are as good as meaningless and your communication destroyed even before you get the chance to make it right. There is never a second opportunity to create a good first impression, so you have to give your audience a feeling that would make them want to listen to you again anytime and anywhere in the future. Let the language your body speaks while are communicating match the words that drop out of your mouth. Make

gestures and move a bit away from the podium once in a while. Look at people when you are having a facial conversation with them (not down or sideways), and don't distract yourself by looking around while communicating with a person. It makes them feel unimportant, and it makes you look undeserving of respect. It's assumed that you are not serious or have little or no idea of what you are talking about. Learn to carry your words with your body language.

9. **Be concise**: We've already commented on this earlier. In addition, pick up your pen, write what you want to be communicated precisely and drop the pen. Even in informal conversations, there are limits to being extreme with one's conversation. Do not bore your audience with long speeches. Make them want you to continue after you have dropped the microphone or pen.

10. **Imbibe the art of listening**: Most good communicators skip this skill sometimes if not all the time. In addition to everything already said, you must be a good listener to be able to effectively communicate with others. You will know if the persons you are communicating with are listening to you if you are a good listener yourself. Show genuine interest in whatever is being said in the course of your communication, listen attentively, take notes if you must, and do not interrupt. This way, people know that you don't just want to speak

and get out of the environment never to be seen anymore but also that you are genuinely interested in what you are telling people about.

11. **Speak effectively**: This might sound dismissive, but it is one of the core skills needed to communicate. When we discuss effective speaking, it cuts across various parts. Effective speaking includes your choice of words, how you say these words, and the way you support what is being said with your nonverbal communication. It is a given that you would need to use a variety of words while speaking. Oftentimes, we use different words for different occasions and even for the same situations most times. The way you would speak to a two-year-old child to give you something he/she is holding will be different than the way you would request something from a grownup. The situations are the same; the only change is with the people you are speaking to at different times. You would need to master the skill of aligning your tone, voice, facial expressions, and pace to your audience. Your voice when speaking at a conference of thousands should be louder than when you are speaking in a classroom. The way you say what you say and the expression exuding from your body tells a lot about your confidence, in-depth knowledge of what you are saying, and so on.

12. **Do not stereotype your audience**: This is very important, especially when one is called to speak in the

capacity of an adviser or a motivator. Oftentimes, people come to speak to an audience with the belief that the majority, if not all, are doers of everything the speaker has come to present. You do not speak to a group of men about feminism and then speak to them like misogynists. It triggers the impression that you have a negatively preconceived opinion about them and that does not sit well both for your communication and for your audience. Instead, when speaking, keep an open mind. Sincerely ask yourself "Am I here to make these people learn about genital mutilation, and its adverse effects on the girl child, or am I here to talk about the continuous increase in the number of genital mutilations and how we all are doing nothing about it?" Even if one of your audience members is an ardent supporter of everything you spoke against, still, speak without being a judge. Your opposer might be convinced by everything you said if only you said what you were called to say and no more.

13. **Consider the perspective of your audience**: You were called to speak or write on a subject because you have a wealth of knowledge in that specific field and because those who invited you wanted you to teach others what you know. It is important that you bring yourself as much as possible to your audience's level. The aim is to ensure that your audience understands all you have to say and not to tell them that you know what you have been

called to say. Break the subject matter down as much as possible to a level that your audience would understand. This is what communication is all about.

It's important to understand that people are mostly, if not all the time, attracted to people like themselves. This is why most of your friends are those who have the same vibe and energy (or lack of energy) as you. It is essential to master people when trying to communicate with them. Survey the environment and test the waters. You cannot speak to a set of university graduates the same way you would speak to a class of school kids if you were to give the two groups of students graduation advice. You should learn to blend into the situation and blend into your audience. If they are speaking softly, there would be no need to go on and on as if one is in an argument. If it is an argument, one would expect you to match the energy of your opponent. Learning to blend into your environment will increase your goodwill relationship with people, increase your market value if you are a marketer, and boost your self-esteem.

An important question to ask is: why is verbal communication important? Why is it important that I am well equipped with the skills of oral communication? Humans are a pack of animals, and so it would be nearly impossible to be able to cohabit with one another without the use of well-defined and restricted set of words. Imagine if there were no words to communicate with, or if the use of words was not regulated. What would it look like if "cat" could be spelled any way provided the letters "a", "c", and "t" are in the spelled word? Imagine if all words meant the same thing, and there was no way to express ourselves in other ways. Humans would have found it very difficult cohabiting. This is because, every day, we yearn to be heard, to make a point, and to pass out to others how we feel. If we go back in history, we find that our ancestors, even in their daily lives, used words to look out for one another. For sustenance, protection and their continuous development, they sought for and used words. It was the basic means through which their existence was justified. This is why if we go back in time, we will realize that the most pronounced persons who led others were people who were notable for their speaking abilities. They were the people who had grown using words and using them well. So, from generations past, words have been important, and it will always remain so. Also, the proper use of words to convey to others how we feel is an important skill without which the world would remain stagnant.

Firstly, verbal communication is important to inform others and to pass down ideas from generation to generation. Imagine the time it took for the documentation on the events of the First and Second World Wars, the happenings of colonization, and other major historical events that preceded the present generation. All of this knowledge would be lost without verbal communication. No one in the present generation would have a close guess to the happenings in generations past if people had not made them available through books and journals. Apart from books, the act of oral verbal communication is very crucial. This is particularly effective for articulation and clarification. People do not get the opportunity to clarify to their audience while communicating if they are doing so in writing except, of course, another person or the same writer reviews or critiques the book. Oral verbal communication, therefore, allows you the opportunity to clear the cobwebs for your audience and also allow them to ask you questions as to what they do not understand. This is more direct than any other form of communication, and it is very important when it comes to the role of informing others through verbal communication.

Additionally, verbal communication is used to correct a wrong. Where words are stronger and more persuasive than actions, this will play out. It is often used during arguments and debates. Oftentimes, we see this use of verbal communication in law courts where justice can be had for even hardened criminals and for those who have committed the crime in question. Although this is the wrong use of this form of communication, it comes very close to explaining how important verbal communication can be. Arguments are not won through gestures or by just giving sign language, and all these constitute examples of nonverbal communication. In extolling verbal communication in this sense, nonverbal communication is also key to the success of your communication verbally. This is because your ability to adjust your tone with the words you use, your ability to maintain eye contact between your audience and your books and, of course, your ability to move one or two steps without losing your poise or the idea or what is being communicated is key, and it will help your audience understand you better.

A species social life and entire being are determined largely by what they communicate and how they communicate it. There are no limits to the use of words or to the number of words present today or to the number that would evolve in the future. Humans do not remain stagnant. It is in our nature to want to grow and fend for ourselves. We also move around, and in the process, communicate. It is a definite part of our everyday lives. So, it is important to learn how to blend into every situation, all the while communicating.

Chapter 3: Direct and Indirect Communication

Direct and indirect communication styles are two of the most prominent communication styles that exist. A communication style refers to the way humans make use of their different languages to communicate with others.

Direct communication is a process of communicating whereby the person speaking says exactly what they have in mind. There are no mincing words. One of the remarkable features of direct communication is active listening. The party being spoken to pays a great deal of attention to what is being said and also gives feedback when necessary. Because direct communication involves active listening, it makes it that what exists is a sort of two-way traffic between the two parties communicating.

The essence of direct communication is to convey exactly what is meant by the person speaking. As a result of this, the person does not lace his/her words with innuendos or try to incorporate hidden meanings into what is being said. When you are trying to imagine direct communication, what should come to mind is the expression "Honesty is the best policy." This is because the aim of direct communication is achieved when the purpose that the speaker has in mind–which could range from having a grievance addressed to even just explaining a concept to a person–is effectively conveyed to the recipient.

One of the advantages of direct communication is that it actually proffers solutions. This means that whatever it is that the speaker has in mind would be better achieved, and the speaker better served, when direct communication is employed. There is no pouting, gesturing, or any other such indirect communication style employed.

Furthermore, direct communication makes the entire system of processing and analysis of the information by the recipient easy. When words are spoken, the person being spoken to has to receive the information, then move further to process the information received to make sure that the intended message imbued in the spoken words make sense and result in the intended outcome. A receiver's work is made a lot easier when the speaker is frank and direct. This will mean that the words will be taken at face value, and when this sort of culture is continued, there will be an enhanced system of communication and feedback between the parties.

In direct communication, short, sharp sentences are mostly employed. The expectation is for the speaker to get right to the point of what is being said, and short sentences are the best ways of making sure that that is the case.

The communication style that is employed by a person usually depends, to a large extent, on the cultural ties that the person has. Specific cultures have certain accepted norms and the mode of communication is one of such norms. For instance, if a person is raised in a family where the adults or role models in the home bottle up their feelings and cannot speak freely about whatever issues that they have, they will grow up with that mindset, and it would not be uncommon to find this person remaining with this mindset even to his own family or the workplace.

The schools and social circles also contribute to a person's concern as to what is an acceptable style of communication. These two mentioned locations are the primary areas of socialization for the child and have a huge impact on the development of the child–including what is taken to be the acceptable style of communication, whether direct or indirect.

A distinction, for the purpose of determining the style of communication employed by a person, is made between low-context cultures and high-context cultures. Low-context cultures refer to cultures that are diverse. These cultures place a huge emphasis on individualism and the independent development of the child. Furthermore, a person who has primary socialization as part of a low-context culture will typically come in contact with many diverse people as he grows up. As a result of the aforementioned reasons, people who are a part of a low-context culture are wont to engage in direct communication. Direct communication, for them, comes as a matter of necessity as they strive to make certain that whatever they have in mind is effectively revealed to the recipient. Also, it would be difficult for any individual from a different culture to appreciate fully any innuendos or hidden meanings when a party is speaking. Direct communication is the best way of exchanging messages between individuals who are not part of the same culture.

On the other hand, persons who are from high-context cultures tend to engage in indirect communication. These individuals are usually found within cultures that have some sort of homogeneity. Thus, the absence of diversity makes it so that the party will be unaccustomed to dealing with those who do not share the same ideals with him. An example of a high-context culture could be some cultures found in Africa and Asia. From the given examples, it can also be inferred that apart from the homogeneity that is found within such cultures there is also the fact that deference and respect are often touted by these groups. Direct communication may be considered rude and thus inappropriate. This sort of socialization is also carried over by the individual from their private lives to their social communications and even the workplace.

In the workplace, direct communication should be the prominent mode of communication. However, even with this knowledge, many people still find it difficult to have direct communication in the workplace. The question is then this: how can you make use of direct communication in the workplace? Firstly, you have to understand that with direct communication, the focus is on the other party. Both parties are supposed to focus on understanding each other's perspectives. As is with communication generally, direct communication would have been achieved when there has been a transfer of the intention of the speaker to the receiver. What this means is that when engaging in direct communication, you are supposed to pay less attention to speaking than to actually making sure what is said is being understood.

Also, if the purpose of the communication is to find an amicable solution to a problem, both parties are also supposed to talk through the problem. At this point where a solution is being sought, it is irrelevant whose fault the problem is. Particularly in a workplace situation, both parties are expected to suspend whatever bias they hold to make certain that the problem is handled and a solution is given.

You have to keep in mind that direct communication does not mean that no background information should be given concerning the topic. Direct communication entails engaging the subject head-on, but for that to be possible, background information has to be provided so that the other party can gain perspective about the subject. When this is not done, the other party becomes defensive, and this defeats the whole essence of the communication. As a matter of fact, this could even escalate the situation further than it already is.

Finally, if you are talking to a peer and there is some sort of power imbalance between the two of you, then you need to tread more carefully. Direct communication can come with an air of haughtiness, so you have to make sure that you dispel this while speaking to your peer. As stated earlier, the whole essence of communication, whether direct or indirect, is to make certain that information is received and processed between both parties. Whenever you create a condition where this is not possible, then you are hampering the process of communication.

Advantages of Direct Communication

Subsequently, we will be doing an analysis of the direct versus indirect communication styles; however, at this point, it is necessary for us to discuss the advantages of direct communication:

1. It is very effective: If you have been following the discussion, one thing you must realize is how effective direct communication is. Effectiveness can never be overemphasized because the world as we know it depends on making sure that communication is carried on well. There is hardly any segment of the human experience that would function smoothly if there was a lack of some form of efficient communication. That is why direct communication is all the more important. Direct communication is the most effective means of communication because it provides the best way of learning what a person has to say. Granted, it is possible that words may have double meanings and also that conversations, when taken out of context, would hardly make sense. However, the truth remains that when

compared with the other modes of communication, direct communication provided the safest bet for the actual transfer of information.

Direct communication also provides actual solutions to any issues that are raised. What this means is that in an environment where the solution to any issue is being sought, the best means of achieving such is through direct communication. If your intention is to get an employee to tow a certain path, or even if you are trying to express grievances to a superior, the most effective means of making that happen is through direct communication.

Furthermore, direct communication ensures that there is feedback from the person being spoken to. This will help to ensure that what is said is understood by the other party and also makes sure that there is compliance with what has been discussed. In trying to gauge the response rate, direct communication is the best means of doing so.

Direct communication is also very important, especially when compared against the statistics that show that spoken words contribute to less than 10% of all communications between humans.

2. Trust is better created with direct communication: When you look people in the eye while speaking with them it goes to enhance the level of trust the person being spoken to has for you. Evasiveness (beating about the bush) may

give the impression that there is something you are trying to hide. Also, when you develop the habit of addressing any issue that arises and making your thoughts clear on any subject, people around you will feel a sense of predictability, and this will increase the truth they have for you. If you are leading a group of people, regardless of how small the group is, then you will realize how very important it is for you to make sure that people on your team get to trust you.

3. Direct communication can be an excellent way of forming bonds with people: one of the aims that can be achieved through communication is the creation of a relationship with others. In this sense, direct communication is one of the best ways of creating any such relationship. The reason for this is that in a vast majority of cases, direct communication involves a face to face conversation with the other party.

The truth is that it is often necessary to form bonds and create relationships with the people around us through communication. The relationships could range from romantic to coworker relationships in the workplace. In any of these instances, direct communication will help you achieve that. As already pointed out earlier, direct communication causes people to trust you. When you are frank and direct, people will look to you to give the correct assessment of any problem at every stage and this helps open the door for the creation of relationships between you.

4. Direct communication protects confidentiality: There are situations when what is being discussed is highly confidential and there would be a requirement that the parties discuss the issue without divulging the contents. Whenever this is the case, direct communication is excellent. Direct communication makes sure that whatever that is being discussed stays between the two persons and does not spill over to a third party.

Indirect Communication

Indirect communication refers to the process whereby a person chooses to "act out" what they have in mind instead of being express with their intentions and thoughts. In indirect communication, the speaker relies on their tone of voice, facial expressions and gestures to convey their thoughts. Typically, the reason for engaging in indirect communication is to save face, either for the person speaking or for the other party. Furthermore, indirect communication could also be a means of avoiding conflicts and arguments. Here, speakers rely heavily on nonverbal cues, trusting that the other party could interpret what is being said (or unsaid) and give the appropriate response required.

Indirect communication is commonplace is high-context cultures. As pointed out earlier, this is because these cultures foster environments where there is interdependence between individuals. People often learn some societal cues that may not be understood by people outside of that particular social circle. Thus, there could be distinct knowledge of what is acceptable or not, what is right or wrong, certain phrases and slang, etc.

In cultures where indirect communication is prevalent such as with the Chinese and Japanese, being direct is taken to be rude, especially when what is being passed across is negative information. In this sort of setting, the expectation will be for evasiveness to be employed in order to diffuse tension and maintain harmony.

Culture, as used above, is used in the broad sense; however, it can also be used to refer to sub-cultures such as the family, church, or immediate community. Although these larger groups often exert some influence on the smaller groups, they, however, evolve their own sets of rules of what is acceptable or not.

Benefits of Indirect Communication

From all that has been discussed, it is almost as though the advocacy is for people to make use of direct communication styles, as opposed to the indirect style. However, is there any benefit to be achieved from speaking indirectly? Or, to put it in proper perspective: are there circumstances when it would be ideal to communicate indirectly? Definitely.

In the first place, indirect communication can help you prevent embarrassment. Also, indirect communication helps prevent you from putting yourself and the other person in an awkward position. In indirect communication, the speaker can make adjustments to his content. The speaker reads the cues from the listener and then decides the best approach that can be employed to pass the message across. Thus, when the speaker realizes that something he intends saying would be harmful or may not achieve the intended purpose, he could quickly make adjustments and in that way everyone benefits.

Indirect communication may actually make you a good communicator. Indirect speakers are very likable because they take the feelings of others into consideration while speaking and people tend to appreciate that. As a result of this, people may be more willing to communicate with indirect speakers than direct ones.

Furthermore, indirect communication introduces you to some sort of exclusive club. If you are good with indirect communication, you will be able to communicate effectively with others. It is actually easier to be a direct communicator than it is to learn the ropes on us to be tactful and empathetic while speaking; traits which are found more in indirect communication. You will also be more equipped to interpret cues from other indirect speakers. Even when a person is not saying anything audibly, you could read the nonverbal cues from the person and interpret what is not being said.

Differences Between Direct and Indirect Communication Styles

If you have followed the discussion up to this point, then you will definitely have an idea of the differences that exist between direct and indirect communication. However, for the purposes of emphasis, I will just briefly point them out.

In the first place, direct speakers speak their mind. When they are trying to settle an issue, they go straight to talking about what the problem is. For the indirect speaker, he will most likely look for ways to make it obvious to the other party that he is offended without saying so outrightly.

Direct speakers are not afraid of confrontation. In fact, it might even be argued that by the method they employ they actually court confrontation. This view may not be entirely correct because when a direct speaker is speaking, his intention is for the problem to be quickly addressed, and the focus is not on offending the other party. On the other hand, indirect speakers try to avoid confrontations so they will most likely choose a route that will not lead to conflict.

Direct speakers ask for immediate feedback and do not lead room for any sort of misconception. In direct communication, the speaker expects the other party to give feedback regarding whether the message passed across has been received. This is because the aim of every direct speaker is to get the situation resolved as soon as possible. In indirect communication, rather, there is room for miscommunication because the indirect speaker relies heavily on nonverbal cues. The person being spoken to may not interpret the nonverbal cues correctly and may lose the whole essence of what is being said.

Finally, direct speakers often get the issue resolved faster than indirect speakers. When you have an issue that you need to resolve as quickly as possible, your best bet should be direct communication. It is for this reason that it is usually advised that in the workplace what should be employed is direct communication. This is especially so if the emphasis is placed on achieving results and not necessarily on building a stable relationship between the speaker and the listener. A direct speaker will sacrifice the possibility of maintaining peace if the job will be done, even if some coldness develops between both parties.

On the other hand, indirect communication is ineffective when trying to resolve issues. In the first place, the listener may not even realize the full extent of what is being discussed due to the fact that the indirect speaker does not get straight to the point. Also, the indirect speaker often withdraws whenever the discussion gets heated and emotions get stirred. In the end, the issue does not get to be fully resolved.

Chapter 4: Tips for Effective Direct Communication

Now that we have discussed what direct communication is and the benefits of making use of it in day-to-day relations, the next step will be to explain how one can improve their direct communication skills. This is because, no matter how well you know the benefits of direct communication, you will never really get to experience them unless you are applying the principles effectively. Below you will find some tips that will be helpful in improving your direct communication.

Learn to disagree without stirring up conflict. It is almost impossible for humans to exist if conflicts in one form or another did not exist. Furthermore, due to differences in idiosyncrasies and perception, it may be hard to avoid conflicts when in conversations with others. More so, direct communication may seem confrontational, especially when employed by a person who lacks the capacity to effectively manage conflict. So, as can be seen from the foregoing, there is a great chance that you may enter into conflicts with the other party while in direct communication with them. The key here then is to seek for ways to minimize the chances of conflict arising, or even when they arise, looking for effective ways of tackling the conflict without losing the substance of what is being said.

The first means of avoiding/managing conflict while engaging in direct communication is pausing. Before you go straight to saying something to another person you need to actually pause and make sure that you have a proper perspective on the issue at hand. Following this, you also have to make sure that you fully understand the situation. It will hardly make sense if you move headlong into directly speaking with a person if you do not understand the full extent of what is going on, even in the instances where the direct communication is a conversation, you also have to be sure that you are paying attention to the other party. As stated earlier, direct communication is predominantly done face-to-face, and this means that you will be physically present with the person with whom you are directly conversing with. Hence, to be an effective speaker and to make sure that conflict does not arise, you have to make sure that you understand the other party fully.

You have to learn to redirect the conversation at any point when you notice that emotions are getting heightened. Redirecting is a skill you should learn to be a good communicator. You should learn how to diffuse the tension by changing the topic of discussion. The idea is to make the transition smooth and not make it obvious that there was some tension as a result of what is being discussed.

Develop the habit of asking questions. A lot of the conflicts that arise from direct communication stem from the fact that the speaker does not often give the other party opportunities to clarify certain things. Direct speakers often go straight to what the perceived problem is even when they may not have the full picture. You have to make sure that that isn't the case with you. Always ask questions. Always give the other party room to give explanations, and if necessary, make amends. The problem is not with the fact that you will be frank and direct, but make sure that you do so after the person has finished giving the answers to your question. Explanations will give you a better understanding of what the issue is, and you will be able to channel your anger directly at the proper persons.

Finally, always be ready to let go. A lot of issues may not even arise in the first place if you are willing to let go in certain situations. Before you barge in and say whatever you want to say, always ask yourself if it would be better to let the matter go. If it will be better to let go, then do so.

Chapter 5: How To Merge Direct and Indirect Communication Styles

Experts have revealed that one of the biggest problems people have is the ability to merge the direct and indirect communication styles. This is especially so when the parties communicating are from two different cultures and are used to different expectations. For instance, in countries such as the United States, Australia, Germany and the likes, the emphasis is placed on going straight to the point and being frank with whatever that is being said. In these cultures, it would be confusing if the person speaking is being indirect. They may fail to grasp the full extent of what is being said because they'd be unable to interpret the cues sent from the other party.

On the other hand, in the indirect communication style, speakers would often choose the route that is less likely to cause conflict between the two parties. While being direct is considered respectful in the countries mentioned above, in Asian countries such as China, being indirect is considered to be the hallmark of respect. So, when an individual finds himself in a location where there is a mixture of people from the two different cultures, how does he navigate the space without being offensive in his communication? The key is in merging both the direct and indirect communication styles. The tips below can be employed to make sure that you enjoy a smooth sail while doing so:

- Acknowledge first that there is no right or wrong way of communicating. The fact that the communication style that you are used to different from what the other person employs does not make yours superior or vice versa. You just have to make peace with the fact that the differences exist and that it should not hamper your relationship with the other party.

- You also need to admit that it may take a lot more work for you to effectively communicate with the person. However, it is not impossible. When you acknowledge the amount of work that you have to do, you will be better equipped to handle the task head-on. It will, of course, make sure that the level of frustration that you encounter during the entire process is reduced also.

- You have to realize that you may have biases. For instance, direct communicators may think that indirect communicators are evasive and dishonest. Indirect communicators, on the other hand, may think that direct communicators are rude and without empathy. You have to acknowledge that you may have biases, and you should also make sure that you set those biases aside. They are usually biased because they are not true. For instance, what the indirect communicator may consider being rudeness may just be the individual being frank and direct, and what the direct communicator considers to be evasiveness could just be that the individual was trying to be respectful. You have to acknowledge that you may already have some bias, and you need to work on them.

- Finally, you need to empathize with the other party. You have to put yourself in the shoes of the other person. This will help you understand why they will most likely respond in a certain way and will also help you become more flexible. You also have to make sure that you pay attention to how others may choose to show respect and how that may differ from what you know. Respect is a universal concept that is valued in every culture; the problem arises when you fail to understand how a party chooses to show theirs.

In your workspace, you also have to be very careful about the communication style that you choose. For instance, it may be better to employ an indirect communication style than a direct one. This is because priority may be placed on harmony in the workplace over blunt comments, even though the later may produce more results. It will also be very important for you to pay attention to nonverbal cues.

Also, if you are an indirect speaker you have to realize that the nonverbal cues that you give may not be interpreted the way you expect them to be. You also have to understand that the other party most likely will appreciate your honesty, and this will be valued more than respect.

Chapter 6: Nonverbal Communication

Nonverbal communication involves all the processes of sending and receiving messages without the use of written or spoken words. Nonverbal communication is the most popular of the different types of communication that exists. It is highly steeped in informality, and it is possible that you would be employing it without even knowing. For instance, once you step into a room, you immediately send signals to everyone around you, and the signals would implant in the minds of others and communicate something–either in the positive or negative–about you.

Nonverbal communication was introduced into mainstream usage by the psychiatrist, Jurgen Ruesch in the book, ***Nonverbal Communication: Notes on the Visual Perception of Human Relations***, which he co-authored with Weldon Kees. From that time, nonverbal communication has come to be accepted as a very important aspect of human interactions. It has been stated that more than half of all active communications between individuals are nonverbal. This brings to mind the huge impact nonverbal communication has in the lives of everyone around. Nonverbal communication is very important in the world today, (the importance and place of nonverbal communication will be better discussed later on.) However, it still has the potential of being misinterpreted, such as where what is being said is lost and a different meaning is obtained.

Importance of Nonverbal Communication

Knowing what to say is only half of the job. The real task is in saying it effectively and achieving the desired results. In this vein, nonverbal communication is excellent in achieving the latter. It makes sure that not only do you have something tangible to say but that what is being said is coherent and clearly understood by the other party. Here are some of the reasons why nonverbal communication is important:

1. Nonverbal communication is excellent for disclosing a person's emotional state: Verbal communication may not be effective in conveying to others how you feel about anything or how deeply something affects you. However, this could be expertly conveyed with the use of nonverbal communication. You will be able to show the other party how you feel by the use of facial expressions, hand gestures, etc. More importantly, it helps provide feedback to the other party. Even while you are engaged in verbal communication, nonverbal cues could be the means of informing the other party that you are either listening or that you are not listening to what is being said by them. For instance, when being spoken to, a smile could be a way of telling the other party that you are listening to them. Also, when you shake your head vigorously, it could alert the other person to the fact that you disagree with them and will thus give them the opportunity of clarifying.

2. Nonverbal communication is very honest: People do not have conscious control of their nonverbal communication the way they do for their verbal communication. What this means is that someone could be saying one thing verbally and mean something entirely different based on their facial reaction, hand gestures, or body posture. That is why it is often advisable to follow the nonverbal signals given by a person over anything they are saying verbally.

Governments all over the world pump a lot of money into studies that try to classify people based on the nonverbal cues that they give off. These studies are especially helpful when it comes to detecting criminals or profiling terrorists. Nonverbal communication helps security agents to determine potential terrorists based on the signals received from them. In the situations where these sorts of profiling are successful, they go a long way in averting disasters.

3. Nonverbal communication makes it easy for the message to be understood: Nonverbal communication is universal and can be interpreted by persons regardless of where they are from. This is unlike verbal communication, which can only succeed in locations where there is some uniformity in language. When nonverbal communication is employed, it is easier for the listener to understand and interpret the message. The interval between the message and the reception is also very small compared to verbal

communication. Noticing and interpreting nonverbal communication gives you an edge over the other party.

4. Nonverbal communication is excellent for establishing human relationships: As earlier mentioned, individuals may not be entirely honest with whatever they say. However, it is seldom possible to hide your true intents when engaged in nonverbal communication. Nonverbal communication helps in building trust between the speaker and the listener. When what is verbally said matches the nonverbal signals being given off by the speaker, it creates a culture of trust between both parties.

Researches are being carried out each year to determine the impact of nonverbal communication on human relationships and from what has been found, it has been established that we communicate as much as 93 percent of our beliefs and ideals through the use of nonverbal communication.

5. Nonverbal communication is important for revealing a person's personality: Personality is like the total aggregate of a person. It encompasses all the phases of a human, including the mental, physical, and emotional states. Personality encompasses all the signs of the psychological state of a person and so can be very helpful in revealing whether a person is happy or sad, depressed, angry, or withdrawn. All of these are traits that can only be revealed through nonverbal communication. So, even

when we may not be able to distinctly tell a person's mental state, we can make informed calculations based on how the person has been communicating with us.

From this, it can be seen that nonverbal communication can also help increase efficiency at the workplace. It can be very helpful in interview sessions. You can reveal to the interviewer whether you are confident, bold, capable, etc. simply by the nonverbal cues that you give off. It is very important to learn how to make use of nonverbal communication very well to make sure that the quality of your work does not suffer as a result of that.

6. Nonverbal communication is very helpful also for handicapped persons who may not be able to effectively make use of verbal communication. In fact, in some instances—such as where a person suffers a speech impairment—nonverbal communication may be the only means through which they could communicate. It is also very important for illiterates. Although we are constantly striving to eradicate illiteracy in the world today, there is still a huge part of the human population who can neither read nor write. It would be difficult to communicate with people who belong to this class if the person cannot make use of nonverbal communication skills.

There is no overemphasizing the place nonverbal communication has in our world today. Given the nature of our society today and the ever-changing landscape we are in, there is a need to have a firm grasp of the nuances and the subtle hints that people give. In the corporate world, for example, something as trivial as how a handshake is given might be determinative of how the individual will be viewed. Also, certain cultures abide by certain rules. Western cultures appreciate the frankness and will expect that a person maintains eye contact during conversations. However, this is not the same with certain cultures such as the Japanese's. If your business will necessitate your interacting with people from diverse cultures, then you have to learn how to adapt in every situation.

Disadvantages of Nonverbal Communication

As previously mentioned, one of the drawbacks of nonverbal communication is an inability to understand what is being spoken. This is just one of the numerous disadvantages that could exist with the use of nonverbal communication. The others are:

1. It does not work for everybody: No matter how effective nonverbal communication is taken to be, there are people who will still feel comfortable with verbal communication, and for these people, nonverbal communication will simply not cut it. Also, it may not be ideal in every environment. For instance, in certain formal environments, the expectations would be for a speaker to

say verbally what exactly they want to say. In those sorts of situations, nonverbal communication may not be ideal.

2. Nonverbal communication is imprecise: A lot of meanings could be attached to a simple gesture such as a wave. Also, given the context in which it is done, a smile could elicit happiness, dread, or repulsion from the other party. There is no scientific way of determining what is meant by a person making use of nonverbal communication. Thus, it could lead to extreme confusion if the listener cannot be sure of exactly what the speaker meant by an action he performed.

Furthermore, it may be impossible to stop nonverbal communication. With verbal communication, the speaker only needs to stop talking or writing for the communication to come to an end. However, with nonverbal communication, the conversation can still be ongoing even when the speaker has stopped speaking.

Furthermore, it is possible to tell when the subject of verbal communication has changed. When the speaker moves from one point to the other, the listener can tell. However, this is not the same as nonverbal communication. With nonverbal communication, the listener will be unaware when the subject matter has changed or when the speaker intends to say something different than what he had been saying before.

3. Multi channels are used during nonverbal communication, and it may be possible to be lost trying to keep up: In typical nonverbal communication, the speaker may be communicating with different parts of their body at the same time. They could be smiling, and at the same time, gesticulating with their hands. If a person focuses on only one of these at a time, it is possible that they will miss out on what is being said from all the other sources. This is not the same with verbal communication where there is just one channel of communication being employed. In nonverbal communication, there is the absence of explanations that may be really necessary for the proper understanding of what is being said.

Types of Nonverbal Communication

1. **Eye Gaze**: The way a person looks at a person or a thing can convey a great deal about them. Of course, there are certain instances when a person can look at another and it would be considered offensive. In some instances, maintaining eye contact can be taken as a sign of honesty. Thus, a person who cannot meet the eyes of the person he is speaking to is taken to be insincere. Also, research has revealed that when people see what they like, there is an increase in their blinking.

2. **Haptics**: Haptics is the scientific study of touch and is one of the most important nonverbal communication techniques. Studies have revealed that the amount of touch a person receives as a child can determine how well they turn out in the future. In the same vein, people who do not experience positive touch, even as adults, have more mental and physical health issues than the others. Hugs, kisses, embrace, etc. are some of the ways touch can be used as a vehicle to communicate different feelings from one party to the other. The amount of touch a person is allowed on others is usually determined by what is socially acceptable in that clime. In most cultures, women are less averse to touching each other in social situations.

3. **Appearance**: From our choice of clothing, the type of lipstick that we put on, and our hairstyle, all of these could communicate a great deal about us to the other party. There is evidence to show that different colors evoke different reactions and also that perceptions from people can be greatly influenced by how a person looks.

4. **The environment**: The state of a person's immediate environment can communicate a lot about them to others. For instance, the state of your car, or your house could say a lot about you to a person who is meeting you for the first time. It is because of this reason that businesses take a lot of care to accessorize their offices properly. Classrooms are usually painted in dull colors because they are taken

to have a calming effect suitable for learning. Similarly, hotels and restaurants paint their locations with bright colors to give a welcoming feel.

5. **Body Language and Posture**: You may not know it, but you are probably saying a lot simply by the way you are seated and the posture you walk with. There has been tons of research carried on into how a person may be communicating with their body language and posture. The most popular of those is how defensive gestures such as arm folding can have profound effects on others.

6. **Silence**: Silence can be a very powerful nonverbal communication. In this situation, the party says whatever they want to without saying anything at all. At one point or the other, everyone experiences the silent treatment. When we are at the receiving end of the silent treatment, we know that the person is trying to tell us something even though they are not saying anything. Silence tells you that the other person is unwilling to engage in the conversation with you. When it conveys that idea, it is now left for you to inquire why this is the case and also look for ways of correcting that.

Silence could also be used to regulate the conversation. It could signal the end of one conversation and the beginning of another. Of course, there is a difference between comfortable and awkward silence. Also, when silence is hostile, it will be obvious to the other party too. The idea is this: silence sends you a message concerning the position of the other party. Whatever the message is, it prepares you to take the necessary actions to bring about the results that you desire.

Techniques To Improve Your Nonverbal Communication

Now that we have an understanding of what nonverbal communication is and the various types that exist, the next step is to learn how to maximize it so that you pass your message accurately. I had earlier pointed out that one of the pitfalls of nonverbal communication is the fact that messages and signals can be lost while being transmitted to the other person. Therefore, the points I'd discuss below will make sure that you convey the messages you want to convey appropriately. Here we go:

1. Regulate the tone of your voice:

Whenever you are speaking you should be on the lookout to ensure that the tone of your voice is conveying exactly what you want to say. The pitch of your voice should rise and fall to demonstrate emphasis or to show the level of enthusiasm you have for that particular subject.

If you are the listener, you should also pay attention to the tone of voice of the person speaking. It could be an indication that you are bored or that there is something they are keeping from you.

2. Maintain eye contact:

Maintaining eye contact could be an indicator of honesty and confidence. Typically in Western countries, it is expected that you maintain eye contact with the person you are conversing with. While speaking, ensure that there is regular eye contact with the person you are speaking to.

Also, maintaining eye contact when being spoken to could indicate to the other party that you are interested in what is being said. When your eyes wander all over the place, it gives the impression that you are uninterested in what is being said and could make the other party uncomfortable. However, you should learn to moderate your eye contact. Make sure that in a bid to maintain eye contact you do not begin staring at the person and cause discomfort.

3. Be mindful of your posture:

The posture you maintain while speaking to someone is very important. For instance, in a formal meeting, it would be inappropriate to swing your legs back and forth or to drum your hands on the table; it could give the impression that you are impatient and want to leave. Do not slouch; this could indicate disinterest. Also, while walking into a room, keep your spine straight and your head looking right ahead.

Another thing you should learn is to avoid fidgeting. Fidgeting may distract the speaker from what he is saying so you should make sure that you do not do that.

4. Pay attention to context:

Context is everything. Often times, the nonverbal communication will be incomplete if not properly placed within the context of the conversation took place. You have to make sure before you place any importance on any nonverbal signal that you understand the context. This will help you not to misread or misinterpret what is being said.

You have to also pay attention to whether the environment is formal or otherwise. This is particularly for when you are the one making use of the nonverbal signal. It will be necessary that you use the nonverbal signal appropriate for that sort of situation. For instance, it would hardly make sense for you to be waving your arms sporadically in a formal meeting.

5. Give the other party some space.

Part of being an excellent communicator is understanding that there should be an appropriate space between the speaker and the listener. Different cultures determine what is appropriate in any given situation, and you have to make sure that you notice when the other party is getting uncomfortable so as to withdraw.

The essence of what you are saying will be lost if the other party cannot process the information because of personal space issues.

6. Practice: This is fairly simple. For you to get the hang of anything, you have to practice. Following all that has been discussed, you should notice the areas that you need to improve on and work on improving those areas. It may take a long time, but if you put your mind to it you will eventually get the hang of communicating effectively with nonverbal signals.

Chapter 7: How Learning Effective Verbal and Nonverbal Communication Can Improve Your Influencing and Persuasion Skills

We have discussed what verbal and nonverbal communication is and how they are important in everyday communication. We will be moving a step further to analyze how effective use of the two means of communication can improve your persuasive abilities.

In some instances, communication transcends just the provision of information and gets to the point where the aim is to get the other party to agree to your own view regarding anything. So, why is it necessary to master the two types of communication to increase your persuasive abilities?

Firstly, where there is a disconnect between the verbal and nonverbal cues the listener will find it difficult trusting you. When what you are saying does not correlate with the nonverbal signals that you are projecting, the listener will be able to tell, and when they do, they will think you are dishonest. This is particularly important because trust is the cornerstone of persuasion. You cannot convince anyone if you have first not gotten them to trust you. Thus, a mastery of the two skills influences your ability to generate trust.

Furthermore, when people have any doubts about what you are saying, nonverbal will be the means to validate or dispel their doubts. This, take for instance that you are trying to sell a commodity to someone, and the person has preconceived notions about said product and is trying to make up their mind whether to trust you or not, beyond what is being said, the nonverbal cues will either convince the person or not.

Furthermore, a firm grip on the techniques to be employed in verbal communication will help increase your persuasive skills. Every great salesman is a great verbal communicator. They know just the right words to use in certain when to steer the conversation toward another direction and also how to make use of nonverbal cues to convince the other party. You should know that the greatest weapon in your armory is words, and if this is so, wouldn't it make the greatest sense for you to polish them often?

Finally, humans are inherently emotional creatures. We make decisions based on our emotions even before we become rational about them. Thus, the greatest way to convince anybody is to tug at their emotions. Great verbal and nonverbal signals will help you achieve this. Great verbal skills will make sure you say what ought to be said, and the nonverbal skills will make sure that you back the words up with the appropriate gestures and signs to achieve the best results.

Chapter 8: Types of Nonverbal Communication

From time immemorial, people have been communicating without using words of mouth or written words. In our world today, there are too many forms by which people communicate without using words. In our day to day activities or even anywhere that we relate with people, be it in our places of work, school, market, and others, we can determine the feelings of people by their gestures without having them telling us anything. These nonverbal communication outlets help one in reading or understanding the activities, situations, and people around in any environment. The types of nonverbal communication are listed below.

1. Kinesics nonverbal communication.

2. Haptic nonverbal communication.

3. Personal appearance.

4. Vocalics and paralanguage.

5. Distance or proxemics.

6. Silence

Kinesics Nonverbal Communication

Kinesics is among the most common forms of nonverbal communication used by many people. It is a type of nonverbal communication that involves the use of gestures, head posture and movement, facial expressions, eye contacts, and other body movements. Gesture can be defined as a motion of the limbs or body, especially one made to emphasize speech or expression. The motions or movements can be in the forms of waving your hands to signal "goodbye" or even "hello," signaling someone or people to "come" by stretching your hands and making the tips of your fingers touch your palm at the same time, keeping your first finger on your lips to signal "no talking." Just in the same manner, you can use your hands to indicate the shapes and sizes of objects; if it is a small or big one, the space between your hands and sometimes, the forms you keep them are enough to indicate the volume of the said object. The hand gesture can also be used to describe the height of a person, an object or even an animal. If the height is tall, average, small, short one; we keep our hand or hands at the level that will describe the estimated height of what or who is involved. When you enter a classroom or anywhere that learning takes place, and you see a teacher teaching, the gestures that the teacher employs goes a long way in determining the level of attention that the teacher will get from the learners. A teacher who stands at a particular spot with hands by the side, stiff and standing at attention, will hardly get good attention from the learners. On the contrary, a teacher that teaches and makes gestures that suits what is being taught, will not find it hard to get the due attention of the learners. Gestures, most especially those done by hand, are mostly used by influential public speakers since they have mastered the art of using it. When properly used, it enhances learning, gets the people entertained and draws attention to you. Hand gestures are frequently used to make emphasis, buttress certain points, make a sort of persuasion since it has to do with almost everything about sensitivity. Using gestures also shows the level of your confidence. When you are talking to someone or a group of people, and your hands are shaky, it shows you are not confident about what you are saying or you are just timid. In another case scenario, when you are communicating and your use of hand gesture is topnotch, people will listen to you and they will be more likely to adhere to whatever information you are trying to pass on. It is noteworthy to say that people are more interested in your display of gesture than the words coming from your mouth.

You may ask why? It is because you may not find it hard to fabricate all sorts of lies and tell them, but your gestures may be the pin that will burst you like a balloon. This gesture is a backup to your speech; in the sense that it has its own way of communication even when you are doing the same orally. Gestures are very necessary for communication because even people with speech difficulties rely on it to communicate with people even to the point that they do engage in businesses. They use their hands to make certain movements or signs, which expresses their thoughts.

When talking about gestures, the American Sign Language easily comes to mind. It is expressed by movements of hands and face, and serves as a medium of sending and receiving messages for the deaf, dumb, hard of hearing and also, some people who hear and speak very well, especially in places where there is the need to maintain silence.

Head posture and movement as a form of kinesics. When you ask someone a "yes or no" question, and the person shakes his head, what comes to your mind? When the person responds with a nod, what does it tell you about the question asked? From time immemorial, people of different cultures, races and traditions have accepted nodding of head as a form of agreement to whatever it is that the speaker is talking about; on the contrary, shaking one's head is also a form of signaling "no" to any issue at hand. Before a child starts to speak, the child will first try nodding and shaking the head to convey thoughts and feelings. It is important to note that this is an inborn trait in every sane human being. When you are talking to someone, and the person adjusts his head toward you, what does that signal? It shows interest; the person is interested in what you are saying.

But if the opposite is what you are faced with, and the person draws his head backward, it is a signal showing a lack of interest, it is a display of indifference. Again, bowing your head when you don't intend to greet, sometimes signifies tiredness, boredom, sadness, and other feelings related to that. Using the hand or hands to support the jaw shows the person is having deep thoughts, weak, forlorn and lost in action. Apart from the use of gestures, facial expressions are also another common nonverbal communication method. Actually, whenever we converse with people, we are most likely to observe the looks on their faces. Facial expressions convey the emotional state of an individual to observers. While we converse with them, the words we don't voice out do convey themselves through our facial expressions.

This also has to do with whether you are comfortable with the current discussion, situation, or you don't feel comfortable at all so you needed cutting out from it. The level of trust you have for the individual you're conversing with can be detected through the facial expressions you make. A smile on your face is a good indicator showing that you are happy while a frown is there to show sadness, disapproval, or even worry. These facial expressions do reveal whichever way we are feeling in the sense that by mere looking at the face sometimes, one can easily tell if the expression is that of happiness or the opposite, sadness.

Other feelings that can be deduced using this method include ecstasy, joy, love, admiration, fear, surprise, disapproval, grief, disgust, boredom, interest, anger, vigilance, contempt, confusion, and others. The concept of facial expression is universal, it applies to every culture, race or tradition in the sense that a smile is a smile and it is a feeling of happiness and satisfaction whether in Angola or in Zimbabwe; the same applies to a frown.

Facial expressions can be shown by moving the mouth (wide, closed, or open), nose (relaxed or wrinkled), eyelids (lowered or raised), forehead (raised or lowered) and the cheeks (pulled back or up).

Do you know that the level of your intelligence can be judged based on your facial expressions? Research has proven that people who usually smile are more confident than their counterparts who hardly do the same. Just like the face is the index of the mind, the eyes are the windows of the soul. They have a high propensity in revealing the state of one's mind. Do you know that viewing the images of someone you find attractive can elicit a nonverbal response of eye dilation?

This is because oxytocin and dopamine go to your brain when you are romantically attracted to someone; the surge happens to make the eyes to dilate. In response to some psychological feelings such as surprise, attraction or fear, the pupils do dilate. It is very good to take notice of someone's eye movement and signals when you are conversing; you should try to focus on the size of the person's pupil, if it is dilated or not, if the person is making direct eye contact, looking somewhere else, looking at the ground, blinking too fast, and other things that can indicate how interested they are in what is going on.

People show interest in a conversation if they are looking directly into your eyes. In addition to this, when they take too much time to look at you like that, sometimes, it shows they are trying to suppress you. If they throw their gazes elsewhere periodically, it shows they are being distracted or they are trying to hide something from you. When it comes to blinking, of course, it is natural that we humans do blink; but when the blinking is a rapid one, it shows that the person is uneasy. On the contrary, if the blinking is less, it shows that the person is trying to control his eye movements, sometimes, tears.

During an interview, it is very important that you make good eye contact since this shows the level of your confidence and self-esteem. When engaged in public speaking, making good eye contact shows you are connected to the audience, increases your understanding of them, makes you rapport very well and gets an immediate response; that is to say, if they are listening, interested, bored, or worried. Positions and postures that people do take is a good indicator for knowing the state of their mind. Crossed arms and legs, standing with hands placed on the hip, tapping fingers rapidly, and having the hands placed at the back all have something or things they identify. When you are conversing and you notice that the person's feet are turned toward you, it indicates an interest in what you are saying; if it is sideways, most of the time, it signifies indifference. In the same vein, if the person is sitting upright, it indicates an interest in the ongoing discussion. While hunching the body forward indicates indifference and boredom.

Haptic Nonverbal Communication

According to Wikipedia, haptic communication is a branch of nonverbal communication that refers to the ways in which people and animals communicate and interact via a sense of touch. Touch or haptics, from the ancient Greek word "haptikos," is extremely important for communication; it is vital for survival. It is very important that you should be cautious of every touch you make, especially to someone you are not so emotionally close to. When you touch someone inappropriately especially intentional, you are most likely to be punished, and most of the time, a legal punishment which will have other negative consequences. Touch can be persuasive, welcoming, or even threatening. It can come in different forms like functional-professional, social-polite, friendship-warmth, love-intimacy and sexual-arousal touch. The first, functional-professional can be in the form of a makeup artist, holding her client's face up, touching some parts of the body while making up the client. The same applies to doctors, tattoo artists, barbers, and others.

They have to touch you so that they can give you the professional services you require. Apart from doing their job, touching you in such forms is not usually a friendly one. A handshake, a pat on the arm or shoulder, is a good example of a social-polite touch.

Here, the touch is a lead way to a discussion on a kind of strictly social-polite situation. We use handshake as a medium of introduction when meeting people for the first time, and also to gain trust. When we talk about friendship-warmth touch, it is more intimate, unlike the aforementioned duo. But when they go beyond the right dosage, the relationship will be bargaining for a deeper romantic interest. In the same vein, the under dosage of it is a signal for unfriendliness. When we talk about touch in the direction of love-intimacy relationships, it is commonly found between love partners, family members, and best friends. It can come in the form of holding hands, touching faces, hugging and sometimes, kissing. These touches point out the intimacy between the people; if it is between lovers, it usually gives rise to a sexual-arousal form of touching.

However, it is worthy to note that this concept of touching is not universal; in the Japanese culture it is seen as an extremely rude action when you touch someone, rather than touching, they prefer to bow as a show of respect and affection. People in Latin America usually kiss the other's two cheeks as a sign of greeting and also to show affection. Touch is not only used in a peaceful and serene setting, but it is also used in a violent and combative situation. Just like you see in wrestling, they touch each other, and the touches are not friendly ones. In a physical conflict or fight, a person slaps, kicks the other and throws him on the ground.

People on first dates usually make touches to display their height of interest in the other person. Here, they usually give a pat at the back, which is a sign of abbreviated hug, respond to jokes by tapping the other lightly on the arm, making their legs touch. When one of them is not interested in the touches, the person is most likely to cross the arms and not return them. Touch here is often returned to show interest; but if you choose not to do it, that is just up to you.

Personal Appearance

Another type of nonverbal communication you should know is personal appearance. Personal appearance is the way you look both in and out of your house. This has to do with your dressing, adornments, pieces of jewelry, and accessories. It is the way that people see you based on your dressing, makeup, hairstyles, bag, suitcase, shoe, grooming, and others. This is a physical view of you from the crown of your head to the sole of your feet; it is actually a communication outlet on its own. The clothing you put on, be it casual attire, suit, professional ones, cultural outfits, uniforms, the styles the clothes are sewn into, their sizes, whether they are tight, fitted or loose on you, the colors and so many other things are enough to communicate effectively on your behalf. When you see a man or woman wearing a lab coat and stethoscope, you don't need anyone to remind you that the person is a doctor or medical practitioner.

Likewise, when you see a person wearing the type of wig you see in courtrooms, and dresses the way people there do, no one needs to tell you that the person is a lawyer. The same goes for a bride and groom on their wedding day. That day, the couple will look different than every other person, most especially the bride since she will be the only one dressed in a spectacular white wedding gown. Our outward appearances speak of our inward sentiments and moods, when you go to a funeral, you will see most people there, wearing black dresses and that shows that they are mourning.

For instance, two people came for an interview in a corporate organization. The first person was dressed in a suit; well-ironed and neat, while the second was simply on jeans, a casual top, wearing slippers and carrying a sling bag.

By mere looking, which one among them do you think will get the job? The first person, well-dressed in a suit will get it because his dressing alone, shows that he is confident and suiting for the job. The other individual may be screened out because of his dressing because it is the first thing to be noticed.

Clothing differs from culture to culture. In some places, women are not allowed to display any part of their body apart from their fingers and feet; they cover very well. While in some other cultures, women are free to wear whatever they like and are free to expose certain parts of their bodies. Your physical appearance is descriptive, and it tells on you. The physical appearance of a seducer is different from that of a nurse and also differs from someone that is dressed in mourning clothing. Since this aspect of you sends messages about you, you should always be neat, dress well, conscious of your image and not just that, spend extra time and money to look presentable and maintain a good image.

Vocalics and Paralanguage

Vocalics or paralanguage is another form of nonverbal communication. Paralanguage and vocalics have to do with voice. Paralanguage is said to be the nonverbal elements of speech, and to a limited extent of writing, used to modify meaning and convey emotions such as pitch, volume, intonation, voice quality, speech rate, loudness, speaking style, rhythm, fluency, and stress. Paralanguage can come in the forms of gasping, clearing your throat, change of tone, whispering or shouting, emphasizing certain words, speaking slower or faster and others.

When someone offends you and is apologizing, it is expected that the tone behind the apology will be soothing and not so loud. The tone, display, and every other thing go a long way in telling us how sincere or untrue the apology is. When a child offends you, and you wish to correct the child by increasing your voice to point out his erring. This child will discover that this is not the way you do talk to him at other times, so he will understand by the pitch of your voice that he offended you so deeply.

Distance or Proxemics

Distance or proxemics is another factor to consider here. Proxemics refers to the distance or space between people as they interact. When a stranger stands or sits too close to you, you will find out that you will not be comfortable there. Proxemics is also one of the forms of nonverbal communication. The distance you wish to have in a classroom differs from the one you have with a coworker, also, from the one you have with the members of your family or even close friends. The level of distance in a closer and intimate relationship will be different from the aforementioned ones. The distance you maintain with people shows how close you are to them, and also the way you relate with them.

Silence

Silence is a kind of nonverbal communication that has nothing to do with words or articulation before passing a message. If you have ever been given the "silent treatment" by anybody, you would agree that several thoughts ran across your mind. What meaning did you eventually deduce from the silence?

Silence is a powerful nonverbal communication that may indicate that someone has chosen not to communicate with you.

Apart from showing a lack of interest in communication, silence can be used to control how a conversation flows. There are other meanings attached to silence. Just as it is with other kinds of nonverbal communication, the context in which it is used determines how silence will be interpreted.

Chapter 9: How To Read Nonverbal Cues

Nonverbal cues are louder than verbal speech. The ability to read and understand them is of utmost importance as it guarantees more effective communication and better relationships. Paying close attention to one's body language enables the communicator to pick up on unspoken issues or problems and discover proper means of handling and dealing with these hints, whether they are positive or negative. From the close examination of the different forms of nonverbal cues, it is easier to formulate an adequate and practical system for recognizing and understanding all forms of nonverbal communication. However, it will still be imperative to critically examine the efficient and effectual means of reading and transcribing nonverbal cues.

Body Language

Body language refers to nonverbal signals that transmit feelings and intentions. It encircles all modes of nonverbal communication. That is facial expressions, position, gestures, etc. A great number of persons have mastered the fine art of controlling their facial expressions. But sometimes, under close observation, they unconsciously and involuntarily make some facial expressions that betray their emotions and thoughts. Smiling is an important nonverbal cue to look out for; it could either be genuine or forced thus sanctioning friendliness or wariness.

A genuine smile majorly engages the entire face, especially the eyes, while a forced smile engages only the mouth and usually communicates dissatisfaction, disapproval or disgust. A half-smile is a common facial expression conveying sarcasm or uncertainty. Tight, pursed lips also indicate displeasure, while a relaxed mouth indicates a relaxed attitude and a positive mood. Other body languages include tapping of feet to demonstrate impatience, twitching of fingers to indicate shyness, and unsteady movements or traipse to show discomfort or anxiety. Disengagement or unhappiness can be communicated by arms folded in front of the body, minimal or tense facial expression, little to no eye contact, sitting slumped with head downcast, gazing away from the speaker, fidgeting, writing or doodling. What is necessary in reading these cues is paying adequate attention to avoid and spot an unengaged audience. Picking up negative body language is a key requirement for effective communication as it helps enhance awareness of people's reactions to certain words and actions.

With regards to head movement, the speed at which a person nods their head illustrates their patience or lack of one. Slow nodding depicts intrigue or fascination with the subject matter of the discussion and fast nodding describes impatience, inattention or disregard for the subject matter of discussion. Tilting of head sideways is also a sign of engagement while tilting of head backward shows skepticism or mistrust. During speech presentation, where the audience nods their heads, it proves agreement with the facts or opinions presented and where they shake their heads, it shows disagreement and dismissal. People draw attention to objects or other persons by pushing their head forward and toward the animate or inanimate thing, they seek to draw attention to.

Like the feet, the hands and arms expose important nonverbal cues. Hands in the pocket can illustrate anything from restlessness to deceit. Hands on the head show frustration or grief, and hands raised above the head portray surrender.

During communication, a person may wave their hands to strengthen their point. Holding the head in one's hand is also a symbol of concentration. When making hand gestures, a person will generally point in the direction of someone with whom they have a relationship with. Hands held out is a nonverbal cue for both acceptance and rejection. Hands placed on the hips is a common gesture for fatigue and indifference. Hand gestures generally provide tips on reading nonverbal communication and attention should be paid to it. The arms are viewed as the doorway to the body. In some cultures, crossing arms while communicating with a dominant character is seen as disrespectful. Generally, arms crossing could represent shock, disbelief, or it could be a defensive and blocking gesture. They equally indicate vulnerability or intolerance; arms raised high is often interpreted as pride and arrogance.

Proximity

As explained earlier, when we discussed posture and distance being nonverbal cues, the distance between two people is fundamental to establishing the relationship that exists between them. It also helps in understanding the sort of intimacy and understanding shared. Proximity is communicated through the use of space, distance, and body touching. Standing or sitting in close proximity to someone is concrete evidence of rapport or trust. It is customary to see friends, family members, colleagues, or acquaintances maintain a comfortable distance between each other. The concept of "stranger danger" makes it ordinary to avoid being in close proximity with unknown persons as a sign of chariness, dubiety, or distrust. This submission is, nonetheless, subject to the culture, religion, traditional practices of the individuals involved, and even the topic of discussion.

Muslim women are expected to maintain considerable distance between themselves and any male who is not directly related to them. In some environments, ensuring that a considerable amount of space exists between a dominant and subservient person is constituent to proving respect and humility. As between couples in conservative societies, wives are more likely to refuse to be in close proximity with their husbands to appear respectful and enable him to exercise authority. This, however, might appear strange and unexciting to persons in western societies where public display of affection by couples is permitted. Being able to read the proximity cue and interpret correctly is an essential communication skill as one should be capable of decoding the space or distance appropriate in all situations.

Feet and Legs

The position of feet and legs is an efficacious indicator of true intentions. The feet and legs, as to turn signals, indicate where the individual would preferably be and one's readiness or eagerness to move. An example of this was given above under posture as a nonverbal cue. Where a person faces sideways with their feet and legs away from the communicator, it is an obvious sign of lassitude or indifference to the presence or message of the communicator. It could be concluded that any position where the listener's feet are not facing the speaker could be read as a temporary desire to interact with the speaker.

Looking at a person's feet is sometimes an unintentional nonverbal communication. Since most people can perfectly manage their facial language and upper body positioning, important clues are often revealed through the feet. Tapping of a foot slowly while sitting or standing could show impatience or indecision. Tilting of legs from one side to another could show apprehension or distress. Studying and understanding feet positioning as a nonverbal cue helps ascertain the unspoken intentions of individuals.

Mirroring

This describes mimicking the other person's body language. During interactions, it is instructive to check for mirroring as it is a positive sign that could convey acceptance, admiration, and attraction. Examples of mirroring include where the audience imitates the sitting or standing position of the speaker, taking a sip of a drink at the same time, or tilting of one's head in the same manner and to the same position as the speaker. Mirroring is a natural phenomenon between friends and people of equal status, and it ranges from copying the other person's body language or speech pattern to dressing the way they do.

The most noticeable form of mirroring is yawning. One person starts and the rest follow. Couples who have lived together for a long period of time are often said to look alike as a result of mirroring each other's facial expressions and even intonation or voice inflection. Although a perfect way to form good relationships, mirroring is interpreted differently by individuals that makes it relevant to examine the reaction of the person being mirrored. So, while some may be incredibly flattered by mirroring strategies, others may find it disturbing and desperate. But research has proven that the majority of people are comfortable with being mirrored and having themselves reflected in another. The significance of mirroring is that it creates a relaxed atmosphere and puts the person being mirrored in a receptive and flexible state of mind.

Eye Contact

Eye contact, as already discussed above, is debatably the strongest nonverbal cue. The inability to make eye contact can signify boredom and even treachery where the person looks away to the side. Dishonesty and honesty are weighed with the eyes; the blinking rate could go a long way to show that a person is untruthful. Quick successive blinking shows stress and where it is accompanied with hand gestures, it portrays the character of the person as unreliable and untrustworthy. The direction of one's gaze reflects his interest; a quick glance at the door or watch indicates a desire to leave. It had been suggested that looking upward and to the right during communication depicts that the person has lied as people often look up and to the left when making up or creating imaginary and false situations. Looking while talking builds an affinity with the person talking, while listening reciprocates the affinity established. Pupils dilate to show concentration and interest which is a favorable emotion. Avoiding eye contact could also appear as a signal that the communicator is unattractive. Just as in other forms of nonverbal communication, eye contact is determined by cultural and religious considerations. The inability to maintain eye contact is enhanced by poor social skills.

Touch

Touch is a rather carefully employed nonverbal cue. It is an integral component of haptic communication. A sense of touch allows one to experience different sensations from pleasure, pain, heat, or cold. Touch goes from a pat on the back to hugging to show affection or care. It is divided into social/polite touch, friendship/warmth touch, love/intimacy touch, and sexual touch, all cutting across the boundaries of culture and religion. Except in formal situations of polite handshakes and pats, touch is usually reserved for the most intimate relationships. One often ignores every day incidental gestures such as hair ruffling or a stroke of the arm. But they are far more profound. They represent the primary language of friendship and understanding and provide a means of spreading compassion. One's acceptance or openness to touch will depend on the existing relationship and the comfort level of that relationship. Strangers in public transportation strive to create enough personal space and avoid touches. Even in a large crowd, people try to not have unnecessary contact with each other. In the professional sector, a limp handshake may indicate uncertainty and lack of enthusiasm while a strong grip may prove dominance. The body language that accompanies a touch is very material. Where a person cringes or flinches before or after touching or being touched by a person, it is a negative cue. With regard to hugging, a stiff posture or facial expression shows that the hug is unwanted. What is mostly overlooked is familiarity leading persons to touch another without looking to check if such contact is appreciated or not. It is important to be sensitive to personal boundaries and watch for cues when touching or making skin contact with other persons.

Time

The use of time is formally referred to as chronemics. Humans are profiled into monochronic and polychronic. The monochronic group place value on time and see it as a precious commodity. The second group values other things more, like relations. This difference is correlated to cultural differences.

In Western societies, time is very necessary and managed properly. A monochronic profile usually keeps to time, plans ahead and keeps schedules, inflexible with time frames and completes the job within the limited time granted. A polychronic character does the opposite. In direct conversations, the use of time could convey a powerful nonverbal message. Punctuality indicates the patience to wait. The speed of speech indicates how long people are willing to listen. A person who is consistently late may not be organized or meticulous. Importantly, the amount of time one dedicates to a person or thing establishes the height of their interest. Time is a nonverbal cue that if noted, speaks volumes about an individual's personality.

When reading nonverbal cues, it is advisable not to read in isolation as it could result in wrong interpretation and unnecessary complexities. The circumstances of the case and the general mood or attitude of the audience are crucial to translating their nonverbal motives. Religious beliefs, personal values, and customs are fundamental to deciding how an individual would react verbally and otherwise in a comfortable and uncomfortable situation. Observing nonverbal cues augments the ability of the communicator to analyze the cues and compare to confirm or contradict them with uttered statements. Nonverbal cues convey information on intentions, concerns, and personality traits. It is not everything a person thinks or feels that they put into words. Thus, the most important thing in communication is hearing what isn't said.

Chapter 10: How To Improve Your Nonverbal Communication

Nonverbal communication is a form of communication we engage in our everyday life and conversation with everyday people. It sends more information and message than verbal communication ever can. Yet, people spend more time improving their verbal communication—learning a new language, learning how to properly enunciate and pronounce words clearly and smoothly, just as a native speaker would—instead of their nonverbal communication.

Nonverbal communications serve diverse functions apart from passing a subtle message and make communication much easier. Some of the functions of nonverbal communication include:

- **Amplify what is being expressed in words**: Chances are that when you say "Yes," you accompany it with nodding your head to show that you agree with the other person and the times you have said "No" were buttressed by shaking your head vigorously to show displeasure.

- **Reflect the true emotional state of people**: People can tell exactly how you feel on the inside without you having to say a word to them through your facial expression, the tone and pitch of your voice and your body language. When you are angry, your tone is stronger and your pitch is louder when you are speaking to people, even when you hide it from your face that you are angry, your voice will always betray you. You probably must have had to ask a person "Hey, is everything all right?" just by taking a look at them. You can easily tell when a person is bored and uninterested by the way they sit or stand.

- **Tell the relationship between people**: For people in love, it is not uncommon to see them "mirror" each other's expression. They tend to smile at the same time; they face each other and look into each other's eyes when they are speaking to each other. These nonverbal communications between them help them feel more connected and strengthen their relationship. You are more likely to be undisturbed about closing up personal space with someone you are familiar with than a total stranger.

- **Feedback between speaker and listener**: In a public place or a formal setting, you would not want to interrupt the flow of communication by breaking into their speech. The responsible thing to do is you make a certain hand gesture that indicates you want to speak, and the other party gives you a go-ahead by either nodding or give a similar hand gesture. Smiling and occasional nod of the head is a sign that you are listening and paying attention to them and what they are saying. Eye contact also shows you are interested in them and what they are saying. These nonverbal signals pass information in a subtle but clear and gentle way.

- **Controls the flow of communication**: Closing your lips firmly during a conversation indicates that you have nothing else to say, also, gentle eye contact with the speaker followed by nodding your head is a quiet way of seeking permission to speak. These unspoken words make communication go on without having to break or interrupt the speaker or the meeting at any point.

While it is good to improve and work on your verbal communication, it is great to improve and master your nonverbal communication so it expresses exactly what you mean and how you feel at the exact time. It is great to learn about your nonverbal means of communication so that you show how you feel because that is how you feel and avoid people reading the wrong meanings to your expressions, you know, you crossing your legs because you feel like crossing them and not necessarily because you are stressed or irritated.

How Then Do You Improve Your Nonverbal Communication? There are different forms of nonverbal communication and there are different ways to improve individual forms of nonverbal communication.

- **Conduct a personal body language examination**: A body language examination or assessment is to help you study and know the various body language you use. To do this, pay attention to how you use body language over a period of time, say a week or a month. Pay close attention to your posture in meetings or when talking to people generally, your facial expression during official and casual conversations and presentations. Watch and take note of how other people respond to your unconscious body language and how you also respond or mirror their own body language.

- **Examine your emotions and how they are expressed in the physical**: Emotions are formed in the mind, but they do not simply exist in the mind. They seep through the mind and find expression in the body. Certain emotions are felt and released physically within the body. Take time to study the emotions, ranging from anger, boredom, ecstasy, frustration, happiness–you feel throughout this period and make attempts to figure out parts of your body that translate the very emotion you feel. If you feel anxious, you most likely will feel your stomach contract or your palms become sweaty. Your body shows your anxiety by the continuous blinking of the eyes, increased heartbeat, and increased perspiration rate. Different people feel different emotions differently and so, being aware of how much your emotions affect your body can help you be in control of how you express yourself nonverbally.

- **Be more intentional about your nonverbal communication**: Allow your body language to reflect your emotions. When you are happy and on the positive side of the emotion spectrum, let it show in your body language, keep your body open and free. When you are confused and need clarity, ask questions and show your confusion by showing or using a furrowed brow. Don't cross your arms when you are enjoying the conversation and want it to go on, keep your arms open and maintain a smile to show that you are interested and are enjoying the conversation.

- **Mimicry is a part of life.** Learn to put it to good use: In your everyday interaction with people, there must have been certain body language and expressions you have noticed and seen that are helpful in certain conversations, for example, nodding of the head when people agree with somebody or an opinion. You can use such an expression when you are communicating with other people when you have the same feelings and share their sentiments. You can also watch the people you are communicating with and mirror their response to you. If they lean toward you, respond by leaning toward them. If they make rapid gestures, do the same. While you are mimicking and copying other people's body moves, be careful to copy only the right ones and not the negative ones such as frowning, fiddling or crossing the arms and legs.

- **Use gestures that are in sync with what you are verbally communicating**: This is to avoid sending mismatched signals to people. For example, when you are verbally expressing remorse and feel bad for hurting a person, a smile should not be on your face while at it. You don't show remorse or regret by smiling. You ruin the apology by smiling because it shows you do not mean or are not serious about the apology. I mean, who smiles during an apology?

Also, maintain eye contact during a conversation. Avoiding eye contact is an indicator that you are lying or not being honest with what you are saying; it can also mean you are not interested in what the speaker is saying, especially when your eyes are on something else. Maintaining eye contact does not mean you steady your gaze on the other person when you do this as it becomes intimidating and creepy, and you do not want to do that.

- **Minimize the use of your fingers**: Do not point your fingers as it may be interpreted as a threat or aggression. Do not fidget; fidgeting clearly is a sign of lack of confidence and anxiety. You may need time to put yourself together if you just will not stop fidgeting.

- **Nodding of the head is interpreted as agreement with what is being spoken or done**: However, it becomes a problem when you just won't stop nodding the head. We are humans, and it is impossible to agree with everything that another person does or says. So, when you keep nodding your head at every point, it is interpreted as you being uninterested in what is being said and you just cannot wait for the speaker to finish.

- **More than what is being said, what is important is how it is being said**: Your tone and the quality of your voice carry more information than the words you speak. People may forget what you said, but they will not forget the tone of your voice. Do not raise your voice; speak in a low or normal tone. Even when you are provoked, keep the tone of your voice down. "We need to talk" can be interpreted and felt differently by people depending on how it was said. Raising your voice is not only disrespectful but can also be threatening even when you do not mean to. Your tone can convey meanings such as boredom, respect, disrespect, and even hostility. More than the words you say, please pay closer attention to how you say it.

- **Respect boundaries and personal space**: There is a reason it is called personal space. For effective communication to happen, you should have respect for your space and other people's personal space. Sadly, a lot of people even learned and supposedly progressive people do not understand the need for personal space. Being aware of how others feel about their personal space is important, and also knowing what is permissible for different people and cultures as it concerns personal space is important. On the issue of boundaries, it is important to know and learn how far is too far. Most importantly, adjust your personal space and boundaries to suit that of the person you are conversing with. If they come close, lean in and when they drawback, do not attempt to close the gap.

- **Face the people you are communicating with**: Regardless of the setting or the gathering, you are in, people want to have that feeling of being important and treated like they matter. When you face the people you are talking with, it gives them a sense of importance and that they are noticed. Don't just give them a silent glance, look into their face and speak to their faces. Pay attention to them and the conversation you are having. Avoid any distractions; don't look into your phone or elsewhere. Focus on who is in front of you and pay keen attention to them. It is an unspoken sign of respect for them and their time.

- **Smile**: Languages differ according to cultures and countries, but one language is spoken and understood by all. The language called a smile. People who smile often are more approachable and easy to relate with because that is the signal they send by smiling at other people. A smile says, "Hey, I'm open, I'm here you can talk to me." A smile can ease people on your side during an argument.

When you smile during an argument, it shows you are relaxed and calm rather than agitated and angered. A relaxed face or a smile during a presentation also makes people want to listen and hear you out.

- **Have a firm handshake and maintain an upright sitting position**: This sends a signal that you are confident and serious. Sitting up straight puts you in a comfortable position and, thus, makes you well able to pay attention to what is being said. When you are standing, stand upright too, no slouching because when you slouch, it gives an awful impression that you do not care about the person talking to you. Being upright helps you listen intently. Stand erect with your head high. It makes the other party equally comfortable as it shows you are not uninterested or in a rush. When you sit, make sure your feet are planted firmly on the floor and the small of your back is against the chair. A firm handshake exudes confidence.

- **Dress appropriately and be properly groomed**: Appearance has a way of speaking more about a person even before the opportunity presents itself for them to speak. Wear comfortable clothing that are not too fitted or too loose. Wear the right shoes for the right events. If something is wrong with your dressing, it makes you lose focus on the event as it turns your attention to yourself.

Your appearance can either portray you as being organized and in-charge or careless and rough.

- **Practice and don't stop practicing until you get better**: The only way to get better at something is by constant practice. It is by practicing that you improve and master nonverbal communication. Observe and pay attention and see how well you are improving or making progress. Tell trusted friends to take videos of you when you are conversing with other people. Watch these videos and see how you can interpret your own body language and how it matches the words you meant to convey.

Improving your nonverbal communication is important on all levels, even in your everyday interactions. As long as your daily interaction involves humans, the need to improve on your nonverbal communication cannot be overemphasized. Improving your nonverbal communication will help you better engage your audience and keep them interested. It will help you deliver extraordinary speeches and presentations.

Finally, familiarizing yourself with your body language and the effect it has on people and how you deliver your speech or conversation will transform you into a more confident being, which in the long run will transcend into how you interact with the different people you meet on a daily basis.

Chapter 11: Nonverbal Cues That Project Confidence

Appropriate eye contact: The eyes are used to communicate levels of warmth, involvement, and interest. The level of eye contact you make with a person or another person makes with you can show a lot about them. When meeting a person for the first time, it is polite to make eye contact with then for a few seconds while it is termed rude to make eye contact and stare. A confident person would usually look into your eyes for a few seconds, say up to five seconds, before making eye contact with another person in the room. Insecure people usually find it difficult to maintain eye contact with people in the room as they throw quick glances at everybody in the room, which easily sells them out as being unsure. Confident people maintain eye contact because they are sure and secure in themselves; insecure people cast quick glances at people because they are seeking approval and security in the eyes of people. In appropriate zones, eye contact should be made about 40-60% of the time. To know if you show confidence with your eyes, tell a trusted friend to help you keep tabs on how often you maintain eye contact during a conversation.

Firm handshake: You are probably wondering how you can display confidence or the lack of it through a handshake. A great handshake is one that involves full palm to palm contact, shake up and down once or twice while smiling and looking into each other's eyes. People will see you as confident if, when shaking, you firmly clasp their hand and squeeze until you feel their muscles tighten before releasing. Especially in a business or formal setting, you will leave a great positive impression on them. Avoid aggressive handshakes, though; one that is sudden. Also, avoid a detached and limp handshake. Treat people with respect regardless of their gender and avoid passing an inappropriate message through a handshake. Also, regardless of gender, you can be the initiator of a handshake and when you do, make it firm, warm and confident.

Effective and appropriate gestures: Gestures help to accentuate the words that are spoken. They are visible punctuations that project visual meanings to your words. Let your gestures be minimal yet effective enough to pass on your message. Make gestures that are lively and natural. Hand gestures make people listen to you, it makes people pay attention to the flow of your speech.

You don't talk to people and in the process, scratch your hair, touch or pick your nose, scratch your ear or play with your fingers or squeeze your fingers like they are some piece of laundry. These gestures are not only rude and disrespectful, but they speak so loud about your lack of confidence. Also, depending on your audience, avoid being overly expressive with your gestures. Limit your movements and gestures if your audience is more of the opposite sex because it may make you look less credible. In this case, allow the tone of your voice and your posture to do the talking.

For a rule on how to make the right gestures, in the words of Carmine Gallo, "Picture your power sphere as a circle that runs from the top of your eyes, out to the tips of your outstretched hands, down to the belly button and back up to your eyes again. Hands that hang below your navel portrays lack of energy and confidence."

Authoritative posture and presence: When you stand upright, tall and straight, the message you pass across is that which reeks authority, self-confidence, and great energy. When you have and maintain a good posture, you send a signal of authority and leadership. When you are sitting, be seated upright and use the chair arms if there are any. Own the space and take up space. Stand tall and with your feet apart, rest your weight on both feet. One advantage of an erect posture is that it points you out as somebody with something meaningful to contribute to the discussion at hand and because people accept your projections about yourself, you would be seen as a winner, competent and as a confident person when you're standing and sitting position are upright and erect.

Be the initiator of interactions: Call the shots. Be the first to make and maintain eye contact. Reach forth for a handshake. Strike a conversation, be the first to smile at people when they make eye contact with you. Remember to always make the first move. It is better to be seen as more confident than be seen as timid.

Paying full attention: When you pay attention to what people are saying or doing, it tells more about how much you respect and honor their time and the value they bring. Confident people are open to learning, they are secure in their space and, thus, have no reason to fear or doubt the other person. Uncross your arms and legs, incline your toes and square your shoulders and lean in toward people when they are speaking to you or when you are speaking to them. Ignore every distraction and give full attention and energy to the conversation.

Respond to other people's nonverbal cues: You can only know they are sending a nonverbal cue when you complete attention to them. In a more formal setting, listen not only with your ears but allow your eyes to listen to what they are not voicing out. Pay attention to their tone and body language. They have a way of telling you when a person is tired and needs a break, when they agree or disagree with you and also when they need a chance to speak. Responding to their nonverbal cues by allowing others to speak and own the moment shows you're secure and confident, it shows you are not scared of allowing others to shine.

Using the right facial expressions: it is not uncommon for the mouth to say one thing while the face is saying something entirely different. In a conversation, your face is the main point of expression, the highlight of the entire conversation is always seen on your face. You do not only use the face to display feelings and emotions, but you also use the face to control or navigate the course of a discussion. Your facial expression can either encourage the continuation or put an end to a conversation. You may not be able to totally control your facial expressions because they are completely involuntary and unconscious, however, it is up to you to pay attention to your expressions and be aware of what each expression says to people. If you want to show people you are excited and enthusiastic, letting your face to become more animated is a good way to go about it. To show you are interested in a discussion, nod occasionally, give a slight smile and maintain the best eye contact. A calm and collected face is a great way to display power and confidence.

Voice tone and pitch: Apart from your choice of words in a discussion, these nonverbal components of your voice such as tone, pacing, pausing, volume, inflection, pitch, and articulation are equally and sometimes, much more important. Communication is not just about what is being said but how it is being said. People are more likely to want to listen to a person whose voice is clear, warm, relaxed, stern and firm than one whose voice is shaky and stammering, even when they have great, useful information to pass across. You can show how confident you are by dressing right and smiling appropriately while maintaining eye contact, all of these can earn you a swift passage that can be ruined easily with the tone of your voice. This is because it is easier for people to form an opinion about you based on the tone of your voice, they don't even need to meet you physically before they form an opinion. A simple phone conversation is enough to make them decide to want to meet with you or not. This is why it is advised you don't answer the phone when you are not in a good mood and when you do, remember you owe it to yourself to project a positive and the right vocal image. Enunciate words properly, avoid the use of unnecessary conversation fillers, stop unnecessary apologies, sound as confident as you can and be as loud and clear as you can be. Don't shout, and don't speak when you are angry. You may not get another chance to redeem yourself. Be careful and guard against using monotone voice during a conversation as it points you as unfriendly and ending a sentence or a point with an upward inflection may be seen as hesitation on your path. Finally, take adequate pauses during a conversation. Slow down and do not speak too fast. Allow relative pauses in between speech so the listeners can process your words.

Head level and well-positioned chin: A level head is a strong indicator of your capability and confidence. It also helps the tone and texture of your voice as it makes it fuller and clearer. It is also much easier to maintain eye contact with people when your chin is raised than when your head is bowed. A lowered head and chin is a subtle way of you telling people that you are unsure, insecure passive and even guilty of something.

Walk: From the way you walked into a room, people can easily draw their conclusions about your confidence and how much value you carry. A step of confidence (no pun intended) begins with a great posture. Keep your chin up and raise your rib cage high to add confidence to your walk, imagine yourself being tall and light. Keep your weight forward on the balls of your feet, do not settle or relax into each step, walk with a natural and comfortable rhythm, and keep your momentum evenly spaced. A powerful confident walk consists of more arm movement and a longer stride with the head held high.

Visible and well-placed hands: According to Vanessa Van Edwards, "Pockets are murderers of rapport. When someone can see your hands, they feel more at ease and more likely to befriend you. When walking into a room or waiting to meet someone, keep your hands out of your pockets." When both hands are placed in your pocket, it makes you appear uninterested, bored, and nervous. It is okay to place one hand in your pocket as long as the other is making gestures. Keeping your palms visible and open shows openness, confidence and a willingness to connect with others. Keep your fingers clean and well-manicured at all times, to resist the urge and temptation to hide your hands by placing them in your pocket.

Smile: According to Marianne LaFrance, Psychology Professor, Yale University, "Smiling has huge consequences for establishing connections. A smile can improve and repair relationships or ease conflict. It's a way of saying to the other person you can be trusted."

A warm smile when meeting people for the first time creates room for trust and likeability. It also says you feel confident about your body and your oral hygiene. Smiling should be done appropriately and when necessary. Excessive smiling, especially from one sex to the opposite sex, may indirectly point to an ulterior motive and you don't want that. Smile often and be genuine but avoid going overboard with it.

Dress the part: Above everything else, your dressing is the easiest and most obvious part of you that easily sells you out as being confident or insecure. Confident people draw less attention to themselves with their dressing; they want the spotlight to shine on them and not on what they are wearing. They want you to listen to them and what they have to offer and not focus on their physical appearance. How do you tell a confident person from their dressing? Check out their neckline, how plunging is it? Look at their suit, how tight or lose is it? How revealing is their attire? Is their makeup mild or excessive? When you look at them, do you lose focus of what they are saying or you can still flow? Why do you maintain eye contact with them, is it because you are so interested in what they are saying or you want to catch a glimpse of their body? Even when you know your onions, dressing the part still works more magic because apart from you being addressed the way you are dressed, you do not want to deliver a mind-blowing speech and the only thing people can remember from the speech is how beautiful the details on your dress is. Easy with the cologne and perfumes too. Yes, you should smell nice but by all means possible, do not show up to a gathering smelling like you literally had to swim in a pool of perfumes. When you are confident in yourself and in your abilities, you would not strive so hard to draw any attention to yourself.

In conclusion, because other people's perception of us is as a result of what we project to them, I will leave you with the words of Amy Cuddy, the author of Presence "Your body shapes your mind. Your mind shapes your behavior. And your behavior shapes your future. Let your body tell that you're powerful and deserving, and you will feel more confident."

Chapter 12: Mind-Control Techniques

Mind-control techniques exist and can both serve a useful and destructive purpose. The result of using a mind-control technique is directly proportional to the underlying motive of the person engaging the mind-control technique.

Mind-control techniques mean different things to different people. Some people call it coercive persuasion while others call it seduction, coercive persuasion, brainwashing, thought reform, and manipulation. Regardless of what people choose to describe it, they all obviously point toward the same direction; they all point toward the direction of mind-control and how you can influence the mind of an individual to do what you want them to do, to take on a role and play a specific part you want them to play.

A lot of techniques are employed in mind-control to disrupt or alter the mental process of a particular individual. These techniques are quite effective and may have long-lasting effects that are permanent and irreversible. It is worthy to note that not all mind-control techniques are negative and destructive as some have really positive effects.

Generally, mind-control techniques have effects so powerful that they are powerful enough to influence a person's thoughts, beliefs, actions, preferences, choices, and in extreme cases, their whole identity.

Mind-control is very subtle and does not happen fast. It is subtle yet complex and dangerous because the one whose mind is being controlled may not be aware they are being controlled or manipulated. It is dangerous because anybody can be manipulated without them knowing. Anybody's behavior and belief can be altered without them knowing they are being controlled. The interesting part is that anyone can be a manipulator, anybody can manipulate and control your mind, especially those close to you.

The Different Mind-Control Techniques That Exist

1. Isolation: Physical isolation has really destructive effects on people. When people are isolated from their peers, friends, and family, it has an effect on their being, they become fearful, withdrawn and desperate to human affection and attention. Manipulators will always attempt to, first of all, isolate their victims from other forms of human interaction. When physical isolation is not feasible, they attempt to isolate them mentally. This isolation is not done in an obvious manner, it is done in a subtle and unsuspecting way by organizing a week-long camp away from home for their victims. A period long enough to limit any other influence and control the flow of information is all they need.

2. Criticism: The art of criticism is one that is employed to make the isolation of victims more effective. How is this achieved? The manipulators pitch their victims against the world. They make their victims see how the world is against them and is out to stifle their lives and everything they stand for. They then make themselves appear as the ultimate savior and show and give you reasons to make you feel lucky that you are a part of them or that they are talking to you. They can also make you see reasons why you should join them so you could win against the world.

3. Social proof and peer pressure: What is social proof? Social proof is simply a psychological phenomenon in which people believe and accept based on general assumptions that the beliefs and actions of a group of people are appropriate and because everyone in that group seems to "do it," then it is the right thing. This technique is used by manipulators to make a person see the reason why they should do it. Manipulators or mind-controllers who have an already large group can employ this technique to convince one person or an individual who is not sure of the step or action to take. Seeing many others doing that particular thing will simply make him do it.

4. Fear of alienation: This technique works perfectly for a person who is already a member of a manipulative group. When a new person joins a manipulative group, the members welcome him and make him feel loved and special by forming tight friendships with him. These new friendships are oftentimes deeper, more real and better than any form of friendship the newcomer has ever experienced prior to the time of joining the group. They lavish him with affection and rewards that lead to a form of dependency between the victim and the manipulator. When in the future, the newcomer decides to exit the group, he finds it difficult to because he would be lonely and alone in the world outside. So he finds himself staying and not being able to leave the group due to fear of alienation.

5. Repetition: This technique quite too simple and appears insignificant to be used as a tool to control the mind, but when you repeat the same thing over and over again to a person, it becomes familiar and they are able to effortlessly remember it. This technique is one of the most important and simple techniques as all it takes is to drill ideas into the mind of the victims. These ideas may be inserted orally using songs or mantras or written, using symbols or words that they read aloud several times. Remember how you use mantras and words of affirmation to motivate yourself, great. So, if you can motivate yourself through affirmations and mantras, be rest assured that someone may most likely in the future, try to control your mind and manipulate you into behaving and acting in a certain way through the use of repetition. That is if you are not already being manipulated.

6. Fatigue: There is only so much you can do when you are physically exhausted and mentally tired. When you are sleep deprived and fatigued, your mental energy becomes depleted and you become less alert, thus making it easier for you to be manipulated.

Apart from depriving you of sleep, your manipulator can also give their victims and engage them in physical activities that diminish their physical and in the long run, cognitive abilities of their victims such as forced hard labor and tough routine exercises. An abrupt change of diet such as decreased protein intake can also weaken the body and mind of their prospective victim.

7. Forming a new identity: The ultimate goal of manipulators is to make you lose yourself and take on a new identity different and far from who you are and used to be. They want you to take on a new identity that follows all their instructions without questioning them. They make you believe and acknowledge that they are good people who are doing something great, they make you agree and accept that they are fun and interesting, they make you acknowledge their views and opinions are valid. Their aim is to make you accept one thing about them and, before you know it, you see another thing about them and you accept and keep accepting till you find yourself wanting to be consistent with your words and actions that you begin to identify as a member of the group.

8. Advertising: This technique is employed by the media to alter our perceptions of beauty, wealth and perfection. This is seen through the use of picture-perfect models on TV and billboards urging you to buy something ranging from cosmetics down to ordinary beverages. The effect of this mind-control technique by the media is seen by people having a perverse definition of beauty, eating disorders, increased medical procedures to augment the body, self-harming and general discontent and lack of confidence in one's body.

9. Reality TV shows: The effect of this mind-control by the media is that it promotes and encourages children and young adults that they don't need to do anything or be educated, all they need to do is try to be on TV and they can be famous. These reality TV stars are the worst role models anyone can ever think of having, yet, because they are on TV and are famous, they are able to control and influence children to aspire to nothing but to be TV stars even when they have nothing to offer the world except free sex on live TV.

10. Brainwashing: The concept of brainwashing works by first crippling the victim and subjecting them to the authority and mercy of the manipulator. When they are broken and helpless, they are then fed with ideas and concepts that are novel to them. They are isolated and forced to believe their families do not care about then, they are forced to confess and accept the new ideas they are being fed. They are deprived and starved and only rewarded when they accomplish certain tasks that indicate how much they are accepting the new idea.

11. **Conversion techniques:** This is the complete transformation and changing of one's ideologies, beliefs, and identity into entirely new and different ones. It is somewhat similar to brainwashing in that it also takes the form of dirt breaking the victims and making them depend on their manipulator before introducing them to their values and indoctrinating them till they are fully converted.

12. Persuading with willpower: Persuasion is an easy way of controlling and manipulating people's minds. This is used by excellent salespeople and marketers. Willpower is a useful tool in persuasion, and manipulators use it by placing a form of pressure on you, which is increased from time to time. They give you reasons why you should do their bidding, they bring in other people to try to talk you into accepting them, they don't give up and they keep pressing and pushing, using words that convey will. With time, the victim will give in to their persuasion and buy into what they are saying.

13. Sports, religion, and politics: The concept of these as a mind-control technique is in their central theme of divide and conquer. They break people's ability and natural tendency to cooperate for survival and teach them to form teams and be a team for the sake of winning and dominating the other team. Religion, on the other hand, has caused more wars in history due to the brainwashing and conditioning of their followers. Politics have been able to push false propaganda and pitch people against each other by promoting false illusions that blind them to the truth.

13. Power: This is the ability you have that you employ to get whatever you want. Getting what you want may not always be feasible due to other people, but understanding the power you have over them and using it to your advantage is what manipulators do. The use of power involves influencing what people say, how they think, and how they act. The most effective power is that which is used in a subtle way that victims do not know it is being used on them. Understanding how much power you have and how much other people have makes it easier to manipulate them.

14. Propaganda: This is a technique used by those in politics and power generally to control the minds of their subjects. Propaganda works by initiating catchy phrases and slogans that the subjects chant, it creates an illusion of activities carried out at the grassroots, it destroys the character and personality of the opponent and classifies the opponent as negative. It promotes the leader as more competent and trustworthy. It may go a long way to incite violence through the use of words that provoke strong emotions.

15. Drugs: The aim of the manufacturers of these drugs is to own your mind and control your actions by making sure you are hooked on and addicted to it. They make you desire it, they make you crave for it as your life depends on it because your life really depends on it. Of what value is a living being without their mind? These drug companies know better, which is why they keep settling the government and continue flooding the streets with drugs, narcotics, alcohol, and painkillers that do nothing but numb the mind.

Mental control and its techniques can be employed by virtually anyone and anyone can fall victim. Mental control can be used by anyone who wants to manipulate or influence another individual. These above techniques serve different purposes which can either be personal, social, or even political. The goal of any manipulator is to make their victims lose their freedom and ability to think and reason for themselves. It is to make their victims lose their identity and convictions they have built over time.

Mental control is not uncommon among sects, groups, and cults. Their leaders use these techniques to add new members to their sects, indoctrinate and keep their current members active and in the group.

People who lack empathy such as sociopaths, psychopaths, and narcissists are well versed in the art of manipulation and control.

Some other people with a detain amount of power and influence may also control the minds of people within their sphere of influence, such as teacher-student, husband-wife, doctor-patient, parent-child, boss-employee.

Chapter 13: Positive Use of Mind-Control Techniques

Mind-control techniques are not only useful in the manipulation and control of other people. Mind-control techniques can be a good or a bad tool, depending on whose hands it is in.

Mind-control techniques are not only applied or used for negative purposes. They are also useful in other situations as long as they are not invasive and the victims are not being coerced or bullied into accepting. When psychologists deploy these mind-control techniques in the treatment of certain ailments and addictions in their patients, they can be immensely helpful in the health and general life of these patients. These techniques are excellent ways to overcome traumatic experiences, suppress and overcome addictions, boost self-esteem, and overcome suicidal or thoughts that constitute or reek of self-harm.

Simply put, mind-control techniques are not always bad, they only become negative when they are used for selfish purposes.

1. **Visualization**: Visualization as a mind-control tool works perfectly in that when you visualize yourself doing certain things, you find yourself having the strength, the energy and the capacity to work toward achieving that particular success. This visualization technique works for athletes and sportspeople generally. They are more likely

to win when they have already won in their minds. It is easier for them to jump over that bar when their mind has jumped.

2. **Meditation**: This trick of controlling the mind is as old as the human race. Meditation is a way of calming the mind and ridding it off all thoughts, it is a way of allowing peace flow into the mind and allowing calmness into it. Mediation enables your mind to focus on the present and what is most important.

3. **Self-hypnosis**: It is similar to meditation. It allows the mind to focus on only one goal by repeating a mantra that is in line with the goal.

4. **Writing**: Writing has a way of giving things form. When you write down your goals, you give it a concrete form and a life of its own. It becomes easier to track and control when you can hold it in your hands and visualize the words.

How do you identify manipulators? There is really no straightforward way to identify such individuals, but there are traits you should watch out for. They include:

1. **When they are acting all sweet and caring**. This is not to say that everyone who acts all nice and caring around you is a manipulator. This is something to watch out for because manipulators often establish a level of

trust with their victims before they go all out on them. This is also important because anybody can manipulate you, especially people close to you.

2. **When they have a form of authority and power over you**. When they are physically stronger, they are your leader or older than you or they generally possess something that places them on the ladder above you. Remember, power can be misused and abused.

In summary, can you Influence the thoughts of other people? Yes. Can others influence your own thoughts? Yes, they can. It is highly possible to influence others and make them do what you want based on the kind of authority and power you have over them. Is it possible to make them obey and listen to all your bidding without questioning? Yes, there is a possibility of this happening.

So while you may not be able to stop others from manipulating other people, be sure you are not using your influence over them as a tool for control or other self-serving purposes.

Chapter 14: Body Language Myths

By now you understand that, knowingly or not, nonverbal cues are sent and received by all parties involved in every conversation. But some things could still stand in the way of your mastering and harnessing both verbal and nonverbal communication skills. One of such things is an erroneous preconceived notion. Let's discuss a few.

1. **You can catch a liar by noticing how they avoid eye contact**. While it is true that some people, especially children, will prefer to look away from your gaze if they are not being honest, some would maintain eye contact to throw you off. People who have gotten comfortable with lying and are now brazen about it may hold your gaze much longer and more frequently than usual. As such, you shouldn't rely solely on eye contact to detect lies.

2. **You can read a person's mind by reading their body language correctly**. You can, of course, make near accurate guesses as to a person's emotions by observing their body language. But mind reading is attempting to learn why they are expressing such emotions, and that is a different thing altogether.

3. **Smiling and moving your hands during a speech is unprofessional**. Those who accept this as a fact deliver speeches or try to hold conversations with little to

no hand movements or smiling. What results is an unengaging and non-communicative speech.

4. **If the person you're talking to crosses their arms, this implies a resistance to the conversation**. This myth completely ignores the fact that there are any number of reasons why someone would cross their arms. The person could be trying to keep warm in low temperatures. Also, it could be that they just feel like crossing their arms.

In essence, common nonverbal cues should not be taken as definitive proof of a particular behavior or emotion.

Conclusion

When subjects like mind-control and human analysis are mentioned, it is, oftentimes, taken to mean something dark and malicious. As though, the only reason a person would learn human analysis must be so that they can be better manipulators. By reading this book, you must have understood that you're not encouraged to take advantage of anyone.

There are several benefits to learning human analysis. Some of which are; being able to offer comfort even when the other party isn't willing to share their troubles. You would be able to show more empathy than usual. Sometimes, it isn't that who you're talking to has refused to share the burdens of their heart or communicate their thoughts clearly with you. They might be unable to because of the language barrier, or speech impediment. The necessity of possessing the ability to read nonverbal cues in such situations cannot be overstated.

You have also learned the various methods to influence the actions of anyone you wish. Hopefully, this book has empowered you to go out there and take charge.

References

Balogun, S. (2019). Why is verbal communication so important for people? Retrieved

from
https://www.google.com/amp/s/www.legit.ng/amp/1226883-verbal-communication-definition-types-importance.html

Direct communication. (2018). Retrieved from

https://www.goodtherapy.org/blog/psychpedia/direct-communication

Goman, C. (2017). 10 body language myths that limit your success. Retrieved from

https://www.google.com/amp/s/www.forbes.com/sites/carolkinseygoman/2017/11/05/10-body-language-myths-that-limit-your-success/amp/

Indirect communication. (2015). Retrieved from

https://www.goodtherapy.org/blog/psychpedia/indirect-communication

Joyce, C. (2012). The impact of direct and indirect communication. Retrieved from

http://www.uiowa.edu/~confmgmt/documents/DIRECTANDINDIRECTCOMMUNICATION.pdf

Learn how to read and use body language in ways that build better relationships at

home and work. (2019). Retrieved from
https://www.helpguide.org/articles/relationships-communication/nonverbal-communication.htm

Mind-control. (n.d.). Retrieved from

http://changingminds.org/techniques/mind_control/mind_control.htm

Morrow, J. (2011). A 7-step guide to mind-control: how to stop begging and make people

want to help you. Retrieved from
https://www.copyblogger.com/mind-control-marketing/

www.ingramcontent.com/pod-product-compliance
Lightning Source LLC
Chambersburg PA
CBHW061818250726

48657CB00001B/482